THE ATTENTION REVOLUTION

MORE PRAISE FOR B. ALAN WALLACE
AND *THE ATTENTION REVOLUTION*

"A bold little book. Its subtitle is a boast and a lure, echoing the muscular
self-help books that promise to make you better, stronger, faster. *The
Attention Revolution* follows a rigorous ten-stage framework for meditation
described by an eighth-century Indian Buddhist contemplative, but Wallace repeats often that you don't have to subscribe to any particular creed
to experience the benefits here—you just have to do the work."
—*Shambhala Sun*

"Analytical yet practical, Wallace's style conveys
very clear instructions with calm authority."
—*Mandala*

"Attention is perhaps our most precious commodity. Alan Wallace
provides a tutorial of a rigorous form of attention training, *shamatha
meditation*, described in Buddhist texts and practices. Wallace notes
that current interpretations of meditation practices such as mindfulness may not reflect the [Buddha's] original intent. In the current rush
to apply many Eastern traditions to our Western culture, some very
important elements of the original teachings and practices run the
risk of being lost. This careful study is likely to lessen such losses."
—Susan L. Smalley, Ph.D., Professor, UCLA School of Medicine

"Wallace is one of the great Western Buddhist thinkers of our day."
—Howard Cutler, co-author of *The Art of Happiness*

The

Attention
Revolution

UNLOCKING
THE POWER OF
THE FOCUSED MIND

B. ALAN WALLACE, PH.D.

foreword by Daniel Goleman

Wisdom Publications • Boston

Wisdom Publications, Inc.
199 Elm Street
Somerville MA 02144 USA
www.wisdompubs.org

Library of Congress Cataloging-in-Publication Data
Wallace, B. Alan.
  The attention revolution : unlocking the power of the focused mind / B. Alan Wallace.—
1st Wisdom ed.
    p. cm.
  Includes bibliographical references and index.
  ISBN 0–86171–276–5 (pbk. : alk. paper)
  1. Samatha (Buddhism) 2. Attention—Religious aspects—Buddhism. I. Title.
  BQ7805.W33 2006
  294.3'4435—dc22   2005037195

ISBN 0–86171–276–5
First Wisdom Edition
09
5   4   3

Cover design by Laura Shaw. Interior by TL from a design by Gopa & Ted2, Inc. Set in Weiss 11pt/15pt.

Wisdom Publications' books are printed on acid-free paper and meet the guidelines for permanence and durability of the Production Guidelines for Book Longevity set by the Council on Library Resources.

Printed in the United States of America.

This book was produced with environmental mindfulness. We have elected to print this title on 30% PCW recycled paper. As a result, we have saved the following resources: 12 trees, 8 million BTUs of energy, 1,072 lbs. of greenhouse gases, 4,448 gallons of water, and 571 lbs. of solid waste. For more information, please visit our website, www.wisdompubs.org. This paper is also FSC certified. For more information, please visit www.fscus.org.

CONTENTS ● ● ●

THE ADVANCED STAGES: ILLUMINATING AWARENESS

FOREWORD BY DANIEL GOLEMAN ● ● ●

Every contemplative tradition has had its guidance manuals, the precious directions that seasoned practitioners pass on to future generations. Alan Wallace has done us all a great service, distilling centuries of practical wisdom on the path of *shamatha* into an accessible, ready-to-use format, a handbook for a profound inner journey.

Alan is uniquely suited to this task: he holds a remarkable intellectual and contemplative pedigree. When he and I first crossed paths, Alan was a monk in the Tibetan tradition of Buddhism, practicing under the personal tutelage of the Dalai Lama. When we next met, Alan was studying philosophy of science and quantum physics at Amherst College. By the time he got his doctorate in comparative religion at Stanford University, Alan had long been publishing a steady stream of scholarly books, ranging from inquiries into the metaphysics of science to translations of complex Tibetan philosophical texts.

But through all this intellectual pilgrimage Alan was preparing for what may be his true calling: as meditation practitioner and teacher. Over the years he would disappear for months at a time, to practice meditation on retreat in the foothills of the Himalayas or in the high Sierra semi-desert of California's Owens Valley. Along the way Alan began to share what he had practiced, teaching retreats on *shamatha* meditation.

And since leaving his academic post at the University of California at Santa Barbara to head the Santa Barbara Institute for Consciousness Studies, Alan has been catalyzing a landmark research program: he will lead a large group of meditators in a months-long retreat designed to hone their attention to extraordinary levels. In cooperation with neuroscientists at the University of California at Davis, these meditators will be assessed before, during, and after this intensive training, to explore how the highly focused mind impacts the brain.

In *The Attention Revolution* Alan Wallace offers guidance in those same methods. In doing so, he offers a potential cure for the chronic distractibility that has become the norm in modern life, an addiction to splitting our focus between email and iPod, between the person we are with and the one on the cell phone, and between the present moment and our planning for the next one.

Alan's proposition sounds simple but is quite radical: we can steadily enhance our capacity for attention, strengthening this mental ability just as we can our triceps. As with our physique, the key lies in well-aimed practice. This book details with remarkable clarity the specifics of methods that can strengthen the attentional muscle.

Alan has a brilliant talent for simplifying complex material. This small gem of a book summarizes the nuts-and-bolts of *shamatha* meditation into a handy and inviting package. Yet there are libraries of learned treatises unpacking and debating this very method and related territory of the mind. Alan brings a keen clarity to many of the fine points of this vast literature— though for the serious student, there is much more to explore.

As with any contemplative tradition, there is a hidden, but essential, element for progressing along this path: a qualified teacher. Particularly at the higher levels of *shamatha* practice, these instructions have traditionally required additional direction in the form of pith instructions, the crucial details and correctives always given orally, teacher to student, that bring life to the printed page. For those who want to pursue the path Alan surveys here, such a teacher will be a prerequisite.

Yet any of us, as Alan points out, can benefit from improving our powers of concentration. There is a spectrum here, from those with outright attention deficits, to those blessed by a naturally keen focus, to advanced meditation practitioners. No matter where we find ourselves on this spectrum, *The Attention Revolution* offers practical steps for taking us to the next level, and reaping its rewards.

ince the late nineteenth century psychologists and neuroscientists have studied attention, but virtually all their research has focused on people with normal or impaired attention. Many studies have been conducted, for instance, on the attention spans of people watching a radar screen, flying a jet, or playing a musical instrument. These efforts have provided little insight into whether attention can be trained. Neither do they indicate whether attention developed with regard to one activity can be applied to another.

We all know that our ability to focus depends on the amount of sleep we get, the stress we're under, and other factors. And the benefits of focused attention are every bit as obvious as the detrimental effects of attention disorders. Thus the absence of scientific knowledge about healing attentional disorders or developing attention is remarkable. Many scientists simply assume that the human mind is inherently unstable and that little can be done to change this. It is a central argument of this book that not only can we improve our attention spans, we can do so dramatically.

While scientists have tried to understand the mind by means of objective, third-person inquiry, contemplatives for millennia have explored the mind by means of subjective, first-person inquiry. Such investigation into the nature of the mind is meditation, and truly effective meditation is impossible without focused attention. The untrained mind oscillates between agitation and dullness, between restlessness and boredom. Thus the cultivation of attentional stability has been a core element of the meditative traditions throughout the centuries, producing a rich collection of techniques and practices. This rich trove of traditional methods is an excellent place to begin looking for ways to enhance attention.

In the Buddhist tradition, this discipline is known as *shamatha* (pronounced "sha-ma-ta"). Shamatha is a path of attentional development that culminates in an attention that can be sustained effortlessly for hours on end. The explosion of Buddhist teachings and teachers in the West has brought with it myriad benefits to people suffering the ill effects of modern life—anxiety, consumerism, and a break-neck pace—along with the age-old human problems of aging, illness, and death. Whether mindfulness or zen sitting, cognitive approaches like mind training and koan study, or chanting and devotional practices, a spectrum of Buddhist and Buddhist-influenced techniques have been adopted widely in cultures that are not historically Buddhist. Remarkably, however, many contemplative traditions today put very little emphasis on developing sustained attention. Some modern teachers of Theravada Buddhism claim that only "momentary shamatha" is needed for insight meditation, implying that sustained, focused attention is unnecessary. The value of shamatha was recognized in early Chinese Buddhism, but modern Zen does not teach methods specifically designed to develop attentional balance in a sustained, rigorous way, distinct from its other practices.

Tibetan Buddhism, on the other hand, does provide detailed instructions for achieving focused attention. Thus is it is all the more perplexing that among Tibetan Buddhist meditators today, both inside and outside Tibet, very few devote themselves to sustained shamatha practice. Hardly anyone heeds the counsel of the great meditators of Tibet's past, who claim that the achievement of shamatha is necessary for all advanced forms of meditation to be fully effective. A mind easily distracted or prone to dullness is simply unfit for meditation of any kind.

I find it astonishing that the training of attention has been so marginalized both in modern science and in many contemplative traditions. I have written this book in part to help remedy this neglect in the scientific and Buddhist communities. My larger wish, however, is to provide tools for anyone who is interested in training their capacity for attention to its fullest. When attention is impaired, it detracts from everything we do, and when it is well focused, it enhances everything we do. Shamatha practice doesn't require allegiance to any religious creed or ideology. It is a key to mental balance whose benefits are accessible to anyone who perseveres in its practice.

MY OWN STORY

I have been strongly drawn to shamatha since first learning about it in 1972. My enthusiasm for it has never waned, and my appreciation of its importance has only grown over the years.

I became fascinated by the possibility of training attention the first time I learned of it while studying Tibetan Buddhism in the spring of 1972. I was living in Dharamsala, India, at the time, receiving instructions on the Tibetan tradition of mental development from a lama named Geshe Ngawang Dhargyey. Over the months and years that followed, Geshe Ngawang Dhargyey gave many detailed teachings on various techniques for training the mind. But I was especially interested in his instructions on developing focused attention, for I could see its enormous relevance for all kinds of human endeavors, both mundane and spiritual.

The lama's description of shamatha training sounded plausible, and its alleged results were extraordinary. Near the end of his instructions on shamatha, Geshe Ngawang Dhargyey suggested to our class of about a dozen students that we meditate together. We all sat upright on our cushions, intently focusing on the meditative object. We thought it would be a short session, maybe a half hour. But the lama continued to sit, immovable as a rock, as his students began to squirm, our minds wandering and the pains in our knees and backs increasing. Finally, after three hours, he emerged from meditation, a contented smile on his face, and gently commented that this practice requires perseverance.

Throughout the rest of the seventies, I continued my study and practice of Tibetan Buddhism in India and later in Switzerland, studying with many teachers including His Holiness the Dalai Lama, for whom I began serving as interpreter in 1979. After ten years, I wanted nothing more than to devote myself to meditation, and I had my heart set on shamatha. How elated I was when the Dalai Lama, knowing of my yearning to meditate, encouraged me to return to India to practice under his guidance! Due to visa restrictions, I wasn't able to stay in India longer than six months, but I spent almost the entire period in solitary retreat in the mountains above Dharamsala. Meditating from four o'clock in the morning until nine o'clock at night, I immersed myself in ten sessions of practice each day. Once a week, a friend delivered supplies from the village, and every few weeks I hiked down the mountain to consult with His Holiness. During that retreat, I also sought counsel from an experienced recluse named Gen Lamrimpa, who had already spent about twenty years in solitary meditation.

I continued to engage in solitary meditative retreats in India, Sri Lanka, and the United States until the end of 1983, when I felt it was time to reengage with my native civilization. Intrigued by the relation between Buddhism and modern science, I studied physics, the philosophy of science, and Sanskrit at Amherst College. After graduating in 1987, I returned to shamatha practice, this time in the high desert of eastern California. Following months of retreat, I assisted Gen Lamrimpa in leading a one-year group shamatha retreat in rural Washington state.

Following this retreat, I spent six years pursuing a doctorate in religious studies at Stanford University, where I wrote my dissertation on shamatha. Concurrently, I received extensive instruction in the Dzogchen (Great Perfection) and Mahamudra (Great Seal) traditions of Tibetan Buddhism, which provide theories and practices for exploring the nature of consciousness. After my comprehensive exams, I took a leave of absence from academia to practice shamatha for five months in the high desert, this time employing a Dzogchen approach. I considered this my "lab work" to complement my academic investigation. After graduating from Stanford, I taught for four years in the Department of Religious Studies at the University of California, Santa Barbara, and beginning in the autumn of 2001, I devoted another six months to shamatha practice in the same high desert region.

Since 1992, I have worked with various teams of cognitive scientists, studying the psychophysiological effects of attentional training and other forms of meditation. In the autumn of 2003, I established the Santa Barbara

Institute for Consciousness Studies, which is designed to integrate scientific and contemplative ways of exploring consciousness. One of the institute's projects is the Shamatha Project, a one-year residential retreat for thirty people that will involve scientific evaluation before, during, and after the retreat.

ACKNOWLEDGMENTS

This book began to come to light when my old friend Lynn Quirolo tirelessly transcribed various lectures on shamatha that I had given during many meditation retreats. She then edited these raw transcripts into book form, which I then edited further. At this point, another dear friend and colleague, Brian Hodel, stepped in and volunteered his time as a professional journalist to rewrite and polish many sections of the text. It was then submitted to Wisdom Publications, at which point David Kittelstrom gave me much valuable advice for radically altering the entire manuscript, which I did, much to its improvement. David and another editor working for Wisdom, Susan Bridle, made many excellent suggestions to improve this work, and James Elliot offered his valuable assistance in preparing it for publication. So this book has been through many iterations, each one, I believe, an improvement on the last, and I am deeply grateful to everyone who has contributed. It is my sincere hope that it will be of value to those who wish to balance their minds through the cultivation of shamatha and that it may also contribute to the scientific understanding of attention and its potential. I wish to express my thanks to my wife and family for their constant love and support, which I cherish more than words can express. Finally, my deepest gratitude goes to all my Buddhist teachers who have taught me the theory of shamatha and guided me in its practice. To them I am forever indebted with the greatest reverence.

B. Alan Wallace

PUBLISHER'S ACKNOWLEDGMENT

The Publisher gratefully acknowledges the generous help of the Hershey Family Foundation in sponsoring the publication of this book.

F ew things affect our lives more than our faculty of attention. If we can't focus our attention—due to either agitation or dullness—we can't do anything well. We can't study, listen, converse with others, work, play, or even sleep well when our attention is impaired. And for many of us, our attention is impaired much of the time.

People whose attention falls well below normal may be diagnosed with an attention deficit/hyperactivity disorder (ADHD), and the most common treatment for this problem is with pharmaceuticals. The popularity of Ritalin and similar drugs has increased dramatically in recent years, and the United States manufactures and consumes five times more of such drugs than the rest of the world combined. The many detrimental side effects of ADHD drugs are deemed a small price to pay for suppressing the symptoms of attention disorders. This materialistic approach to treating ADHD is enormously profitable for the drug manufacturers, but it is profoundly disempowering for the individuals who become reliant on them. While our culture may proclaim "Just say no to drugs," when it comes to treating attention disorders, the message is "Go for the quick fix."

This is not to say that pharmaceuticals cannot be helpful in treating ADHD. They certainly can, as millions have discovered through their own experience. They may be essential at times, especially to combat severe symptoms. But they don't *cure* anything. They merely suppress symptoms while generating harmful side effects, and even if you don't become addicted, you may develop a psychic dependence on them—perhaps for life. Thus, in clinical cases, drugs can play an important role within the context of a wider set of interventions. But the sooner we can get children, adolescents, and adults off their drug dependence and provide them with methods for maintaining attentional balance on their own, the better it will be.

Our faculty of attention affects us in countless ways. Our very perception of reality is tied closely to where we focus our attention. Only what we pay attention to seems real to us, whereas whatever we ignore—no matter how important it may be—seems to fade into insignificance. The American philosopher and pioneer of modern psychology William James summed up this point more than a century ago: "For the moment, what we attend to is reality."[1] Obviously, he wasn't suggesting that things become nonexistent when we ignore them; many things of which we are unaware exert powerful influences on our lives and the world as a whole. But by ignoring them, we are not including them in *our* reality. We do not really register them as existing at all.

Each of us chooses, by our ways of attending to things, the universe we inhabit and the people we encounter. But for most of us, this "choice" is unconscious, so it's not really a choice at all. When we think about who we are, we can't possibly remember all the things we've experienced, all the behaviors and qualities we have exhibited. What comes to mind when we ask "Who am I?" consists of those things we have been paying attention to over the years. The same goes for our impressions of other people. The reality that appears to us is not so much what's out there as it is those aspects of the world we have focused on.

Attention is always highly selective. If you consider yourself a materialist, chances are you attend primarily to physical objects and events. Anything nonphysical seems "immaterial" to you, in the sense that it doesn't really exist, except perhaps as a byproduct of matter and energy. But if you think of yourself as spiritual or religious, in all likelihood you have been attending to less tangible things. God, the soul, salvation, consciousness, love, free will, and purely spiritual causation may seem far more real to you than elementary particles and energy fields. I suggest that if you were able to focus your attention at will, you could actually choose the universe you appear to inhabit.

Attention also has a profound impact on character and ethical behavior. James felt that the capacity to voluntarily bring back a wandering attention, over and over again, is the very root of judgment, character, and will. Christian contemplatives have known for centuries that a wandering mind easily falls into temptation, leading to sin. And Buddhists have recognized that a mind prone to distraction easily succumbs to a myriad of mental afflictions, leading to all kinds of harmful behaviors. If we can direct our attention away from negative temptations, we stand a good chance of overcoming them.

James also asserted that geniuses of all kinds excel in their capacity for sustained voluntary attention. Just think of the greatest musicians, mathematicians, scientists, and philosophers throughout history—all of them, it seems, have had an extraordinary capacity to focus their attention with a high degree of clarity for long periods of time. A mind settled in such a state of alert equipoise is a fertile ground for the emergence of all kinds of original associations and insights. Might "genius" be a potential we all share—each of us with our own unique capacity for creativity, requiring only the power of sustained attention to unlock it? A focused mind can help bring the creative spark to the surface of consciousness. The mind constantly caught up in one distraction after another, on the other hand, may be forever removed from its creative potential. Clearly, if we were to enhance our faculty of attention, our lives would improve dramatically.

THE PLASTICITY OF ATTENTION

While countless studies have been conducted over the past century on various aspects of attention, remarkably little is known about the plasticity of attention, that is, the extent to which it can be enhanced with training. Given the enormous significance of attention in all aspects of life, this oversight is strange.

One of the reasons for the lack of research in this field may be due to a common assumption that the level of our attention is inflexible. William James wrote:

> The possession of such a steady faculty of attention is unques-
> tionably a great boon. Those who have it can work more rap-
> idly, and with less nervous wear and tear. I am inclined to think
> that no one who is without it naturally can by any amount of
> drill or discipline attain it in a very high degree. Its amount is
> probably a fixed characteristic of the individual.[2]

James recognized the enormous significance of the ability to voluntarily
sustain one's attention on a chosen topic, declaring that an education that
could effectively improve this faculty would be *the* education *par excellence*.[3]
But he was at a loss when it came to providing practical directions for
achieving this goal.

As long as our minds oscillate compulsively between agitation and dullness, wavering from one attentional imbalance to another, we may never
discover the depths of human consciousness. Can the mind be irreversibly
freed from its emotional afflictions, such as craving, hostility, depression,
envy, and pride? Are there limits to our love and compassion? Is awareness
finite and immutable? We know that the mind has powers of healing, which
are sometimes attributed to the "placebo effect," and that it has the capacity to make us ill as well. What other powers lie dormant within human
consciousness, and how can they be tapped? These questions have been
posed by contemplatives throughout history, and focused attention has
been a crucial tool in exploring them.

In the modern world we enjoy unprecedented access to many rich traditions of meditative inquiry. The Hindu and Buddhist traditions stemming
from classical India have made uniquely refined advances in the field of
attentional development. The methods of attentional training described in
this book are drawn from this contemplative heritage and involve various
kinds of meditation practice. And while the techniques explained here come
from the Buddhist traditions of India and Tibet, they will be accessible and
beneficial to anyone who engages in them, regardless of religious or ideo-
logical leanings. As with any skill, such as playing the piano or learning a
sport, we can, through drills, repetition, and habituation over time, develop
capacities presently beyond our reach.

No matter where you are starting from, you can benefit from training your attention. My goal in this book is to provide tools for enhancing attention to people no matter where they are on the spectrum of attentional development. At the basic level, these methods may be helpful for preventing and treating ADHD, which turns even mundane tasks into great hardships. For those with a higher initial capacity, the methods here can be used to maintain better attention in everyday life, and bring greater professional performance, physical health, and emotional well-being. Finally, this book contains methods for rigorously refining the faculty of attention to levels unimagined and unexplored in the modern world and will be of special value for contemplatives seeking to unlock the mysteries of the mind.

Especially in the advanced stages, this book sometimes delves into issues that presume either a background in or a proclivity for examining the doctrinal issues that underpin attentional training within a Buddhist context. Since I have written this book in part to address confusion among contemporary Buddhists about how the Buddha and later commentators taught shamatha and the practical implications of that confusion, non-Buddhist readers may find the discussions tangential to their concerns. You need not be a Buddhist to practice shamatha, and you should feel free to skip over these discussions. Nonetheless, you may profit by examining the divergences that have arisen over the 2,500-year history of this discipline.

TEN STAGES OF ATTENTIONAL DEVELOPMENT

As a framework for the gradual development of attention, I have chosen the most complete and detailed description I have found in any contemplative literature—the ten stages described by the eighth-century Indian Buddhist contemplative Kamalashila in his classic work *Stages of Meditation*.

In a historic debate in Tibet, Kamalashila argued that the thorough purification of the mind requires training in three things: ethics, attention, and contemplative insight. Flashes of insight are valuable, but after the fleeting bliss of such meditative experiences, the dirty laundry of the mind still awaits cleaning. For that, contemplative insight must be supported by a high degree of attentional balance, and this requires systematic training.

This path is detailed with landmarks. By using Kamalashila's outline, we can know where we are, what we should be doing, and what to look for. The ten stages of attentional development are:

1. Directed attention
2. Continuous attention
3. Resurgent attention
4. Close attention
5. Tamed attention
6. Pacified attention
7. Fully pacified attention
8. Single-pointed attention
9. Attentional balance
10. Shamatha

These ten stages are sequential. The stages start with a mind that cannot focus for more than a few seconds and culminates in a state of sublime stability and vividness that can be sustained for hours. One progresses through each stage by rooting out progressively more subtle forms of the two obstacles: mental agitation and dullness. The successful accomplishment of each stage is determined by specific criteria and is accompanied by a clear sign.

THREE TECHNIQUES

To guide meditators along these ten stages, I have chosen from Buddhist teachings three techniques that I have found effective for people in the modern world. These three techniques are the basis for the three divisions of this book. For the first four stages, you should practice whatever method you find easiest. By stage five, the mind is relatively stable, and you can move on to subtler techniques.

For achieving the first four stages, I recommend the practice of *mindfulness of breathing*, variations of which can be found in Zen, Vipassana, and Tibetan Buddhism. Mindfulness of breathing means settling your awareness on the sensations involved in breathing, continually returning your attention there whenever your mind wanders.

Beginning with the fifth stage, I recommend a method called *settling the mind in its natural state*. In this technique, you direct your attention to mental experiences, all the events—thoughts, mental images, and emotions—that arise in the domain of the mind. This method is drawn from the *Dzogchen*, or "Great Perfection" lineage, but is found in other Buddhist traditions as well.

With the instructions for the eighth attentional stage onward, we move on to the still subtler practice of maintaining awareness of awareness itself. The technique is called *shamatha without an object*. Here the practice is not so much one of *developing* attentional stability and vividness as it is of *discovering* the stillness and luminosity inherent in awareness itself.

The training in mindfulness of breathing may be helpful to anyone, including those seeking to prevent or treat attention deficit/hyperactivity disorders. Many people find the second practice, that of settling the mind in its natural state, to be more challenging, but some meditators take to it naturally. Likewise, the practice of awareness of awareness is subtler still, but it may be optimal from the beginning for those who are strongly drawn to it.

You may use any one of the three methods to progress along all ten stages of attentional development, or you may follow the sequence described in this book. How fast you progress will depend on the level of your commitment and the degree to which your lifestyle and environment support such practice.

INTERLUDES

Interspersed with my explanations of the ten stages, I have inserted "interludes," ancillary practices that complement the training in attention. After the explanation for each of the first four stages, I have inserted an interlude on cultivating one of four qualities of the heart: *loving-kindness, compassion, empathetic joy,* and *equanimity*. These practices are especially helpful for balancing our emotions and for opening our hearts. If we know how to work intelligently with our emotions, we can avoid many obstacles that might otherwise hinder our pursuit of focused attention.

Interspersed with the explanations of stages five through nine are interludes on the daytime and nighttime practices of lucid dreaming (drawn from modern scientific research) and of dream yoga (stemming from Tibetan Buddhism). These practices are designed to enhance mindfulness throughout the day and the night, for if our focused attention were limited to the time we spent in formal meditation, the benefit would be minimal.

One of the greatest benefits of a powerful faculty of attention is that it gives us the ability to successfully cultivate other positive qualities. With the powerful tool of focused attention, we can uproot formerly intractable bad habits, such as addictive behaviors or harmful thoughts and emotions. We can use it to develop an openhearted stance toward others and, on that basis, experience profound insights into the nature of the mind and of reality, radically altering our relation to the rest of the world.

GOALS AND EXPECTATIONS

Most people would find their lives greatly enhanced just by attaining stage two of the ten stages. This level of development takes some effort, but it can be achieved by people who are living a busy life with career and family commitments as long as they are willing to set aside some time for meditation. It can dramatically improve the quality of everything you do and make you more resilient in the face of emotional and physical stressors. If that is your goal, there is no problem with using the techniques in this book for that purpose.

However, as noted above, this book is also a guide for people who wish to go well beyond what are considered normal levels of attention. For most people, achieving stage three will require a greater commitment than an hour or two spent each day in meditation in the midst of an active life. The more advanced stages of attentional development are accessible to people who dedicate themselves to weeks or months of rigorous practice in a conducive environment. Progress beyond the fourth attentional stage requires a vocational commitment to this training, which may involve full-time practice for months or years at a stretch.

If you traverse the ten stages of attentional development discussed in this book, the benefits are truly immense. Upon reaching the ninth stage, your mind is finely honed, freed from even the subtlest imbalances. At this point, it is said that you can focus effortlessly and unwaveringly upon your chosen object for at least four hours. At the beginning of this training, meditators are traditionally encouraged to practice for sessions of twenty-four minutes, which is one-sixtieth of a full day and night. At the culmination of this training, you should be able to sustain attention with unprecedented clarity for ten times that long.

According to Tibetan oral tradition, among meditators who are well qualified to embark on this discipline, those of sharpest faculties may be able to achieve all ten stages within three months; those with "medium" faculties may take six months; and those with "dull" faculties may require nine months. Such estimates assume that the meditators are living in a contemplative environment and devoting themselves day and night to this discipline. The reference to sharp, medium, and dull faculties pertains to the level of talent and attentional balance individuals bring to this training. Just as some people are naturally gifted musicians, athletes, and mathematicians, so are some gifted with exceptional degrees of attentional stability and vividness, which gives them a head start in this practice. Others may have an extraordinary level of enthusiasm and dedication to this training, and that will serve them well through the long months of hard work that it entails.

This level of professional training may seem daunting and unfeasible to most readers of this book, but compare it to the training of Olympic athletes. Only a small number of individuals have the time, ability, and inclination to devote themselves to such training, which can appear at first glance to have little relevance for the diverse practical problems facing humanity today. But research on serious athletes has yielded many valuable insights concerning diet, exercise, and human motivation that are relevant to the general public. While the training of Olympic athletes is focused primarily on achieving physical excellence, this attentional training is concerned with achieving optimal levels of attentional performance.

Once the ninth level has been achieved, the meditator is ripe for an extraordinary breakthrough, entailing a radical shift in one's nervous system and a fundamental shift of consciousness. One is now poised to achieve shamatha: one's mind is now marvelously serviceable, capable of being used in a myriad of ways, and one's body also is endowed with an unprecedented degree of suppleness and buoyancy. It is a remarkable achievement, unlike anything one has ever experienced before.

Since the time of the Buddha, when people have asked Buddhist adepts about the nature of their practice, they have commonly answered, "Come and see!" In 1992, neuroscientists studying the effects of advanced meditative practice among Tibetan retreatants explained how they wanted to examine the neural and behavioral effects of meditation. One of the monks responded, "If you really want to understand the effects of meditation, I'll be glad to teach you. Only through your own firsthand experience will you truly know the effects of such practice."

Let's now begin working on the first stage, using the technique of mindfulness of breathing.

THE BEGINNING STAGES:
MINDING THE BREATH

STAGE 1: DIRECTED ATTENTION ● ● ●

The first of the nine stages leading to the achievement of shamatha is called *directed attention*. The sign of having reached this stage is simply being able to place your mind on your chosen object of meditation for even a second or two. If you are trying to direct your attention to a difficult object, such as a complex visualization, this may take days or weeks to accomplish. But if your chosen object is your breathing, you may achieve this stage on your first attempt.

The faculty of *mindfulness* is crucial in shamatha practice. Mindfulness in this context differs somewhat from the way some contemporary meditation teachers present it. Vipassana teachers, for instance, commonly explain mindfulness as a moment-to-moment, nonjudgmental awareness of whatever arises. In the context of shamatha, however, *mindfulness* refers to attending continuously to a familiar object, without forgetfulness or distraction.

The first stage of directed attention is achieved by the power of hearing. According to Buddhist tradition, the most effective way to acquire fresh learning is directly from an experienced, knowledgeable teacher. First you hear teachings, then you follow up with reading, study, and practice. The *power of hearing* refers both to listening to instructions and also to reading about them, especially if no qualified teacher is available.

One of the first signs of progress in shamatha practice is simply noticing how chaotic our minds are. We try to remain attentive, but we swiftly "lose our minds," and slip into absentmindedness. People who never sit quietly and try to focus their minds may remain under the illusion that their minds are calm and collected. Only when we try to direct the attention to a single object for minutes on end does it really become apparent how turbulent and fragmented our attention is. From a Buddhist perspective, the untrained mind is afflicted with attention deficits and hyperactivity; it is dysfunctional.

Like a wild elephant, the untamed mind can inflict enormous damage on ourselves and those around us. In addition to oscillating between an attention deficit (when we're passive) and hyperactivity (when we're active), the normal, untrained mind compulsively disgorges a toxic stream of wandering thoughts, then latches on to them obsessively, carried away by one story after another. Attention deficit/hyperactivity disorders and obsessive/compulsive disorders are not confined to those who are diagnosed as mentally ill; the normal mind is prone to such imbalances, and that's why normal people experience so much mental distress! Such disturbances are symptoms of an unbalanced mind.

These two dysfunctional tendencies seem to be intrinsic to the mind. Hyperactivity is characterized by excitation, agitation, and distraction, while an attention deficit is characterized by laxity, dullness, and lethargy. When our minds are subject to these two imbalances, we have little control over what happens in our minds. We may believe in free will, but we can hardly be called "free" if we can't direct our own attention. No philosopher or cognitive scientist needs to inform us that our behavior isn't always guided by free will—it becomes obvious as soon as we try to hold our attention on a chosen object.

Thus our practice of mindfulness of breathing consists of prolonging our awareness of our breath. While this requires an alert mind, such concentration should not be tense but rather balanced. When we discover that we have become distracted from the meditation object, it may feel natural to clamp down more forcefully, tightly concentrating the mind. You can see this in the facial expressions of people who try to concentrate in this way: their lips become pursed, their eyebrows draw together, and their foreheads become furled with wrinkles. They're becoming concentrated, but like orange juice—most of the fluidity is being drained from their minds! If you want to concentrate for a short time and don't mind the side effects of tension and fatigue, you can follow the above strategy. But if you want to follow the path of shamatha, you'll need an alternative.

I had to discover this fact through experience. During my first extended shamatha retreat, I was filled with enthusiasm. I wanted to take full advantage of the rare opportunity that was before me, for I was meditating in India under the guidance of the Dalai Lama! I had no financial worries, and my material needs were easily met. All I had to do was put the instructions into practice. I threw myself into this training with all my might.

Each morning I would rise at 3:30, except once when I slept in until 3:45 and got upset with myself for slacking off. Enthusiastic I was, but so uptight! The Tibetan manuals on shamatha meditation that I had studied over the years stated that the type of attention needed when one began such practice was "highly focused," so I tried as hard as I could to keep my mind from wandering. Within a matter of a few weeks, devoting many hours each day to meditation, I could sustain my attention on my chosen object for up to half an hour. I was elated to be making such fast progress.

As the weeks went by, however, I found myself becoming more and more fatigued. I was draining myself both physically and mentally, my joy in the practice was diminishing accordingly, and I felt my attention was not developing any further. What was wrong? I was trying too hard. The cultivation of shamatha involves balancing the mind, and that includes balancing the effort exerted in the practice with relaxation.

I think this points to a cultural difference between traditional Tibetans living in the highlands of Tibet and modern people leading fast-paced lives, their senses constantly bombarded by telephones, e-mail, the media, and noise. Years of such existence condition the nervous system and mind in ways that might have been considered torture in rural Tibet. One traditional Tibetan doctor whom I know once commented on people living in the West, "From the perspective of Tibetan medicine, you are all suffering from nervous disorders. But given how ill you are, you are coping remarkably well!" Whether we dwell in Boston, Buenos Aires, Berlin, or Beijing, our minds are conditioned to be more high-strung and engaged in compulsive thinking than the minds of Tibetan nomads and farmers living a century ago. So when Tibetan meditation manuals advise beginners to focus their attention firmly, the instructions are aimed at a very different reader than the average city-dweller in the twenty-first century. Before we can develop attentional stability, we first need to learn to relax.

The meditation instruction that follows incorporates the practice of relaxation along with the instruction on mindfulness of breathing.

THE PRACTICE:
MINDFULNESS OF BREATHING WITH RELAXATION

Our minds are bound up with our bodies, so we need to incorporate our bodies into meditative practice. In each session we will do this by first settling the body in its natural state, while imbued with three qualities: relaxation, stillness, and vigilance.

The Posture

It is generally preferable to practice meditation sitting on a cushion with your legs crossed. But if that is uncomfortable, you may either sit on a chair or lie down in the supine position (on your back), your head resting on a pillow. Whatever position you assume, let your back be straight, and settle your body with a sense of relaxation and ease. Your eyes may be closed, hooded (partially closed), or open, as you wish. My own preference when practicing mindfulness of breathing is to close my eyes partially, with just a little light coming in, and I like to meditate in a softly lit room. Wear loose, comfortable clothing that doesn't restrict your waist or abdomen.

If you are sitting, you may rest your hands on your knees or in your lap. Your head may be slightly inclined or directed straight ahead, and your tongue may lightly touch your palate. Now bring your awareness to the tactile sensations throughout your body, from the soles of your feet up to the crown of your head. Note the sensations in your shoulders and neck, and if you detect any tightness there, release it. Likewise, be aware of the muscles of your face—your jaws, temples, and forehead, as well as your eyes—and soften any area that feels constricted. Let your face relax like that of a sleeping baby, and set your entire body at ease.

Throughout this session, keep as physically still as you can. Avoid all unnecessary movement, such as scratching and fidgeting. You will find that the stillness of the body helps to settle the mind.

If you are sitting, assume a "posture of vigilance": Slightly raise your sternum so that when you inhale, you feel the sensations of the respiration naturally go to your belly, which expands during the in-breath and retracts during the out-breath. During meditation sessions, breathe as if you were pouring water into a pot, filling it from the bottom up. When the breath is shallow, only the belly will expand. In the course of a deeper inhalation, first the abdomen, then the diaphragm will then expand, and when you inhale yet more deeply, the chest will finally expand after the belly and diaphragm have done so.

If you are meditating in the supine position, position yourself so that you can mentally draw a straight line from the point between your heels, to your navel, and to your chin. Let your feet fall to the outside, and stretch your arms out about thirty degrees from your torso, with your palms facing up. Rest your head on a pillow. You may find it helpful to place a cushion under your knees to help relax the back. Vigilance in the supine position is mostly psychological, an attitude that regards this position as a formal meditation posture, and not simply as rest.

The Practice

Be at ease. Be still. Be vigilant. These three qualities of the body are to be maintained throughout all meditation sessions. Once you have settled your body with these three qualities, take three slow, gentle, deep breaths, breathing in and out through the nostrils. Let your awareness permeate your entire body as you do so, noting any sensations that arise in relation to the respiration. Luxuriate in these breaths, as if you were receiving a gentle massage from within.

Now settle your respiration in its natural flow. Continue breathing through your nostrils, noting the sensations of the respiration wherever they arise within your body. Observe the entire course of each in- and out-breath, noting whether it is long or short, deep or shallow, slow or fast. Don't impose any rhythm on your breathing. Attend closely to the respiration, but without willfully influencing it in any way. Don't even pre-fer one kind of a breath over another, and don't assume that rhythmic breathing is necessarily better than irregular breathing. Let the body breathe as if you were fast asleep, but mindfully vigilant.

Thoughts are bound to arise involuntarily, and your attention may also be pulled away by noises and other stimuli from your environment. When you note that you have become distracted, instead of tightening up and forcing your attention back to the breath, simply let go of these thoughts and distractions. Especially with each out-breath, relax your body, release extraneous thoughts, and happily let your attention settle back into the body. When you see that your mind has wandered, don't get upset. Just be happy that you've noticed the distraction, and gently return to the breath.

Again and again, counteract the agitation and turbulence of the mind by relaxing more deeply, not by contracting your body or mind. If any tension builds up in your shoulders, face, or eyes, release it. With each exhalation, release involuntary thoughts as if they were dry leaves blown away by a soft breeze. Relax deeply through the entire course of the exhalation, and con-tinue to relax as the next breath flows in effortlessly like the tide. Breathe so effortlessly that you feel as if your body were being breathed by your environment.

Continue practicing for one twenty-four-minute period, then mindfully emerge from meditation and reengage with the world around you.

REFLECTIONS ON THE PRACTICE

The above, guided meditation on mindfulness of breathing is based on the Buddha's primary discourse on this topic. Here is an excerpt from the Buddha's explanation:

> Breathing in long, one knows, "I breathe in long." Breathing out long, one knows, "I breathe out long." Breathing in short, one knows, "I breathe in short." Breathing out short, one knows, "I breathe out short." One trains thus: "I shall breathe in, experi-encing the whole body. I shall breathe out, experiencing the

whole body. I shall breathe in, soothing the domain of the body.
I shall breathe out, soothing the composite of the body."[4]

As I noted above, in this practice you don't try to regulate the breath in any
way; you simply note the duration of each in- and out-breath. In most
Theravada commentaries on this discourse, the phrase "experiencing the
whole body" is interpreted as referring to the whole body of the breath, that
is, the full course of each inhalation and exhalation. Certainly this is a goal
of this practice, but there is also value in observing the sensations of the
breath throughout the whole body as well.

This is a "field approach" to training the attention. Instead of pinpoint-
ing the attention on a mental image, a prayer, a mantra, or a specific region
of the body, open your awareness to the entire field of sensations throughout the body, especially those related to respiration. The emphasis here is
on mental and physical relaxation. If you constrict your mind and your
body, shamatha training will aggravate the tension you already have. By
settling your awareness in the body, you diffuse the knots in the body and
mind. Tightness unravels of its own accord, and this soothes the network
of the body.

Mindfulness of breathing is universally emphasized for those who are
especially prone to compulsive thinking. As the fifth-century Buddhist master Asanga comments, "If involuntary thoughts particularly dominate your
behavior, then focus the mind in mindfulness of the exhalation and inhalation of the breath."[5] Since nearly everyone living in the modern world is
coping with an overload of thinking, remembering, and planning, this may
be just what the doctor ordered: a general prescription for soothing and
healing overworked bodies and minds.

Although Buddhism generally encourages cross-legged meditation, the
Buddha encouraged his followers to practice in any of four postures: walking, standing, sitting, and lying down.[6] Any of these positions is perfectly
suitable. Not everyone living in the modern world has the same type of
mind or nervous system. If you tend toward excitation, you may find lying
down especially helpful for releasing the tightness and restlessness of your
body and mind. But if you are more prone to laxity, you may simply fall

asleep whenever you lie down, so it may be necessary for you to be upright when meditating.

Lying down can also be very useful for meditation if you're physically tired but not yet ready for bed. In this case, you may not be able to rouse yourself to sit upright in a posture of vigilance, but the prospect of lying down for a while may be inviting. Surrender to your body's need to rest, and use the supine position to calm the mind as well. This likely will be much more refreshing and soothing than watching television or reading a newspaper. The supine posture may be your only option if you are ill, injured, or frail. It may be especially useful for meditation by those in hospitals, senior care facilities, and hospices.

Mindfulness of breathing is great for preparing your mind for mental training, but it can also help you fall asleep. If you suffer from insomnia, the above method can help release tension in your body and mind when you go to bed at night. And if you wake up in the middle of the night and have a hard time falling back asleep, mindfulness of breathing can help you disengage from the thoughts that flood the mind. According to recent studies, about 80 percent of Americans are chronically sleep deprived. So even if all this practice does is help you catch up on your sleep, that's worth a good deal.

AN ATTENTIVE WAY OF LIFE

We are all aware of the way the body heals itself. Physicians don't heal abrasions, and surgeons don't mend bone fractures. Instead, they do whatever they can to allow the body to heal itself—by keeping the wound clean, setting the broken bone, and so on. These are so common that it's easy to lose sight of the extraordinary nature of the body's own healing power.

Normally, when we observe something we *can* control, we *do* try to modify it in some way. But mindfulness of breathing involves letting the breath flow in and out with as little interference as possible. We have to start by assuming the body knows how to breathe better than the mind does. Just as the body knows best how to heal a wound or a broken bone, it also knows best how to breathe. Trust your body. You will likely find that sustained awareness of the breath, free of interference from emotional and attentional vacillations, soothes both the body and the mind. You can observe the healing process taking place before your very eyes.

Mindfulness is useful for overcoming physical and mental imbalances produced by a stressful, wound-up way of life, but you also can use mindfulness to help prevent such imbalances in the first place. Environmentalists talk about "cleaning up after the elephant": the endless task cleaning up industrial contamination, and how a far more effective strategy is to avoid fouling up the environment in the first place. Likewise, mindfulness of breathing can be used to prevent the contamination of our inner environment. It helps us tether the elephant of the mind, and avoid the imbalances that so frequently come with modern living.

The healing of the body-mind has another significant parallel with environmentalist ideas. When a stream is polluted, one may try to add antidotes to the toxins in the water, hoping such additives will neutralize the damage. But the more straightforward and sensible approach is simply to stop the flow of contamination into the stream. When this is done, over time the flow of the water through soil, stones, and vegetation can purify the stream completely. In the same way, rather than adopting any special breathing technique, you simply stop disturbing your respiration with disruptive thoughts and emotions. Before long, you will find that the healthy flow of the breath is restored naturally.

According to Buddhism and other contemplative traditions, mental imbalances are closely related to the body, and especially the breath. Whether we are calm or upset, the breath reacts swiftly. Conversely, irregularities in the breathing also affect our emotional states. During the course of the day, our minds get caught up in a stream of often disturbing thoughts, plans, memories, and concerns. The next time you get angry or sad, elated or surprised, note the rhythm of your respiration. Check it out, too, when you're hard at work, concentrating on the task at hand, or caught in a traffic jam. Compare those breathing patterns with your respiration when you're calmly sitting at home, listening to music or watching a sunset.

When we are dreaming, all kinds of mental processes continue, even though our bodies and physical senses are dormant. Our emotional responses to dreams are just as real, and have the same impact on the body and the breath, as our emotions when we are wide awake. The only break we have from such sensory and mental input is when we are in deep, dreamless sleep. It's then that the respiration can flow without disruptive influences from the mind. I believe this is the healthiest breathing that occurs for most of us throughout the day and night. At the end of the day, we may fall asleep exhausted, but then eight hours later, we wake up, fresh and ready for a new day. All too often, this turns out to be just one more day of throwing our bodies and minds out of balance.

We now have the opportunity to break this habit. We don't have to wait until we're asleep before respiration can heal the day's damage. With mindfulness of breathing, we can do it anytime. Not controlling the breath, we let the respiration flow as effortlessly as possible, allowing the body to restore its balance in its own way.

Simply focusing your attention on the sensations of the breath is directed attention, the first stage of this practice. You have achieved the first stage once you are able to sustain your attention on the breath for even a few seconds. When pursued earnestly, a little mindfulness meditation in the morning or at night immediately brings greater clarity to all activities and provides a natural check on unhealthy habits.

But even if you find this practice helpful, it may be difficult to find time each day to devote yourself to such attentional training. Creating time to balance your mind requires a measure of loving-kindness for yourself. Thus, to be able to make choices that are truly conducive to your well-being, as opposed to merely providing pleasurable sensations, you may first need to cultivate loving-kindness.

INTERLUDE LOVING-KINDNESS

With all the demands upon our time, the prospect of taking more time from the day to devote to meditation can appear to be just one more burden. But I would claim that the reason so many people find no time to meditate is not that they're too busy. We're all doing *something* each minute of every day, no matter how busy or leisurely our lives may be. *How* we fill our days is simply a matter of our priorities. It's only common sense to place a high priority on our survival, making sure that we have sufficient food, shelter, clothing, and medical care, and that our children receive the best education possible. To use an educational metaphor, tasks fulfilling those basic needs are "required courses" of action, and everything else we do consists of "electives." What elective activities fill the moments of our days depends on our values.

Another way of saying this is that, after taking care of our basic needs, the rest of our time is devoted to fulfilling our heart's desires. We may envision this as the pursuit of happiness, fulfillment, or a meaningful life. However we conceive of the purpose of our lives, it will focus on people, things, circumstances, and other more intangible qualities that bring us satisfaction. You have already been alive and pursuing happiness for decades. Pause for a moment and ask yourself: How much satisfaction has your life brought you thus far?

CHOOSING GENUINE HAPPINESS

Many of the greatest thinkers throughout history—from Saint Augustine to William James to the Dalai Lama—have commented that the pursuit of genuine happiness is the purpose of life. In making this remarkable claim, they are obviously referring to something more than the pursuit of mere pleasant stimulation. They have in mind something deeper, a more abiding and authentic well-being that comes from within.[7]

Genuine happiness is a symptom of a balanced, healthy mind, just as a sense of physical well-being is a sign of a healthy body. Among modern people, the notion is prevalent that suffering is inherent in life, that it is simply human nature for us to experience frustration, depression, and anxiety. But our mental suffering on many occasions serves no good purpose at all. It is an affliction with no benefit to us. It is just a symptom of an unbalanced mind.

In our pursuit of happiness, it is vital to recognize how few things in the world are subject to our personal control. Other people—family, friends, busy colleagues, and strangers—behave as they wish, in accordance with their own ideas and aims. Likewise, there is little we can do to control the economy, international relations, or the natural environment. So if we base our pursuit of happiness on our ability to influence other people and the world at large, we are almost certainly doomed to failure. What can we control? What freedom do we really have here and now? Our first act of freedom should be to choose our priorities wisely.

Conative Balance and Evaluating Our Priorities

By looking at what we work for and yearn for—what we spend our time and resources on—we can develop insight into our priorities. The term *conation* refers to our faculty of desire and volition. Conative balance, a crucial element of mental health, is expressed when our desires are conducive to our own and others' genuine happiness. Conative imbalances, on the other hand, are ways that our desires lead us away from mental health and into psychological distress. Such imbalances are threefold: conative deficit, conative hyperactivity, and conative dysfunction.

A conative deficit occurs when we experience apathy toward greater happiness and its causes. This apathy is normally accompanied by a lack of imagination and a kind of stagnation: we can't imagine feeling better than we do now, so we don't try to do anything about it. This robs us of the incentive to achieve greater mental well-being. Conative hyperactivity occurs when obsessive desires obscure the reality of the present. Fantasies about the future—unfulfilled desires—blind us to what is happening here and now. Finally, conative dysfunction is when we *do* desire things that are destructive to our own or others' well-being, and *don't* desire the things that lead to genuine happiness for both ourselves and others. I include "others" here because we cannot cultivate optimal mental balance in isolation from others. We do not exist independently from others, so our well-being cannot arise independently of others either. To flourish individually, we must consider the well-being of those around us. As the Buddha declared, "One who loves himself will never harm another."[8]

The Indian Buddhist contemplative Shantideva comments on conative dysfunction in this way: "Those seeking to escape from suffering hasten right toward their own misery. And with the very desire for happiness, out of delusion they destroy their own well-being as if it were their enemy."[9] In Buddhism, misguided desires are called *craving*, which here means an attraction for something whose desirable qualities we exaggerate while ignoring any undesirable qualities. If our craving is strong, we see the very possibility of our own happiness as inherent to the object on which our mind is bent. This disempowers ourselves and empowers the object of our attraction.[10] When reality breaks through our fantasies, disillusionment sets in. That in turn may lead to hostility and aversion, causing us to now project negative qualities upon the object we once craved.

Finding the Time

To bring all this back to the central theme of this book, one major impediment to training attention is not finding time to do it. And the reason we don't find time to meditate is because we are devoting so much time to other priorities. Some of these priorities center on our basic needs, but many are wrapped up in craving in the sense described above. In desiring the *symbols* of the good life—wealth, transient pleasures, praise, and repu-tation—we may deprive ourselves of the *reality* of living well. The reason we don't devote more time to balancing our minds is that we are betting our lives that we can find the happiness we seek by chasing fleeting pleasures. Psychologists have called this the *hedonic treadmill*,[11] and the first step to escaping from this exhausting grind is to seek a vision of genuine happiness that draws on our own, largely untapped inner resources. This is how we begin to cultivate loving-kindness, first for ourselves, and then for all those around us.

MEDITATION ON LOVING-KINDNESS

Begin by resting your body in a comfortable position, sitting either cross-legged or on a chair. Bring your awareness to the physical sensations throughout your body, breathing into any areas that feel tense or con-stricted. Be still, and adopt a posture of vigilance. Then take three slow, deep breaths, breathing through your nostrils, down into your belly, expanding the diaphragm and finally the chest. Exhale effortlessly, settling your body in its resting state.

Attend to the rhythm of your breath for a few moments, letting it flow unconstrained by restless thoughts and emotions. Settle your awareness in a space of relaxation, stillness, and clarity.

Now, from within this serenity, arouse your imagination with three ques-tions. The first one is, What would I love to receive from the world in order to have a happy, meaningful, and fulfilling life? Some of these things may be tangible goods, such as food, lodging, clothing, and medical care. But other requisites for your well-being may be intangible, such as harmony in your environment, the warm companionship of others, and wise counsel to guide you on your spiritual journey. Bring clearly to mind the things you desire to meet your basic needs. Then allow the yearning to arise: may these authentic desires be fulfilled!

Now pursue this vision for your own happiness more deeply. Clearly see your basic needs being fulfilled, and inquire further into what more you would love to receive from the people around you and from the environment at large. What could they provide you that would help you find the happiness you seek? You may bring to mind both tangible and intangible things, whatever you feel would assist you in fulfilling your heart's desire. Imagine that the world rises up to meet you, here and now, and provides you with all the external support that is needed to fulfill your aspirations.

Each of us is constantly changing from moment to moment, day to day, as our bodies and minds are continually in a state of flux. The next question is, What kind of a person do I want to become? What personal qualities do I want to possess? You are changing all the time whether you choose to or not, so envision the changes you would love to experience in your evolution as a human being. Imagine both short-term and long-term changes. And as you envision the person you would love to evolve into, imagine that this transformation is actually taking place, here and now.

None of us lives in absolute isolation from others, no matter where or how we live. We can't help but influence those around us through both our action and our inaction. We are making an impact on the world, whether we want to or not. The last question you may ask yourself is, What would I love to offer to the world, to those around me and to the environment at large? What kind of a mark would I love to make on the world? Invite this vision into your field of consciousness, embellishing it with as many details as you can think of, and then imagine that this dream is being realized here and now.

Just as you seek happiness for yourself, so do all the people in your neighborhood yearn for their own fulfillment. Expand the field of your loving awareness to embrace each sentient being, human and nonhuman, in your neighborhood, wishing, "May each of you, like myself, find the happiness you seek, and may you cultivate its true causes!" Continue to extend your loving-kindness to everyone around you, gradually expanding your circle until it includes all beings throughout the world, each one seeking happiness just like you.[12]

STAGE 2: CONTINUOUS ATTENTION ● ● ●

For most people setting out on the path of attentional development, the problem that overwhelms them is *excitation*. There are many reasons the mind becomes agitated and distracted. Anger and fear certainly have this influence, and simply living in a noisy, hectic environment can easily destabilize the mind. But most commonly, the coherence and continuity of attention is undermined by craving, or misguided desires.

The general symptoms of a mind prone to craving are dissatisfaction, restlessness, and anxiety. We can try to stifle these unpleasant feelings by immersing ourselves in work, entertainment, talking, or anything else that masks these symptoms. Or we can address the source of such suffering by healing our conative imbalances through the practices of shamatha and meditation on loving-kindness.

Advanced meditators who have progressed along the nine stages leading to shamatha have identified three levels of excitation. The first is called *coarse excitation*, which we typically encounter during the initial stages of attentional training. The second two levels of excitation, *medium excitation* and *subtle excitation*, become apparent only during more advanced stages of attentional training.

When coarse excitation takes over the mind, we completely lose touch with our chosen object of attention. It's as if the mind is abducted against its will, and thrown into the trunk of a distracting thought or sensory stimulus. In the first stage of attentional development, directed attention, the level of excitation is so coarse that you experience virtually no continuity of attention on your chosen object. The mind jumps around from one object to another like a bird flitting from branch to branch, never at rest. Such turbulence is overcome only by persistent skillful practice, cultivating deeper relaxation, a sense of inner ease. Eventually, the mind will begin to calm down and you will experience brief periods of sustained attention, but then you lose it again.

In a way, the practice of mindfulness of breathing is easy. It's not hard to direct your attention to the tactile sensations associated with respiration. At the beginning of the session, you resolve to do just that, yet seconds later your mind is elsewhere. The fact that this is normal doesn't make it any less weird. It's as if you repeatedly lose your mind, then regain it for brief periods, only to lose it again and again. We all seem to be suffering from frequent bouts of amnesia!

In the second of the nine stages, *continuous attention*, you experience occasional periods of continuity, but most of the time your mind is still caught up in wandering thoughts and sensory distractions. Don't be misled by the name of this stage. Continuous attention doesn't mean that you can maintain unbroken continuity for long stretches, but that now and again you can remain centered for a sustained period without completely losing track of your object of attention. However, time and again you will still lapse back into coarse excitation, completely forgetting about the intended object of attention. When you can occasionally maintain continuity of awareness of bodily sensations for about a minute, you have reached the second stage.

The second stage is achieved by the *power of thinking*. The challenge in this phase of practice is to sustain interest in the object, and you can do this by thinking about the instructions between sessions. If you are a seasoned meditator, you have probably found that involuntary, internal commentary on your practice can be an obstacle. Even the ongoing thought, "Here is the in-breath…Here is the out-breath…" can be an intrusion. However, internal commentary can also be useful, especially in the first two stages of shamatha practice; if you're thinking about the practice, at least you're not thinking about something else!

Another way to use the power of thinking to help calm the distracted, wandering mind is to count the breaths. This is like using training wheels when first learning to ride a bicycle. While the practice of mentally count-ing breaths involves a kind of thinking, it can help to simplify the concep-tual mind. Instead of having many things to think about during the meditation, you reduce your thinking just to counting your breaths. It is important, though, that in striving to maintain continuous attention you don't lose your earlier sense of relaxation. The stability of your attention should emerge from a relaxed mind, not work against it. Let's proceed now to a practice of mindfulness of breathing that is especially helpful for enhancing attentional stability.

THE PRACTICE:
MINDFULNESS OF BREATHING WITH STABILITY

Begin this session, as you did before, by settling your body in its rest state, imbued with the three qualities of relaxation, stillness, and vigilance. With your awareness permeating the tactile sensations throughout your body, take three slow, deep breaths, observing the sensations of the breath filling your torso from the belly up to the chest. Then let your respiration return to its natural rhythm and simply be present with the breath for several min-utes, breathing as effortlessly as you can.

With this preparation, you establish a basis in relaxation. Without losing this sense of ease, now shift your emphasis to the cultivation of attentional stability. This is the ability to sustain the focus of your attention without becoming fragmented or derailed by the force of distracting thoughts and sensations. With this aim, instead of being mindful of the various sensations of respiration throughout your whole body, focus your attention just on the sensations of the expansion and contraction of your abdomen with each in- and out-breath. As you did before, note the duration of each inhalation and exhalation, and observe the duration of the pauses between breaths.

Out of sheer habit, unintentional thoughts are bound to cascade through your mind like a waterfall. One way of stemming this relentless stream of ideation is to count the breaths. Try that now, by counting "one" at the beginning of your first inhalation, then attending closely to the sen-sations of the respiration throughout the rest of the inhalation and the entire exhalation. Count "two" at the beginning of the next breath, and continue in this way for as long as you find it helpful. Let these mental counts be brief, so that your attention to the counting doesn't override your awareness of the breath itself. The objective of counting the breath is to insert brief reminders into the practice—remembering to remember—so that you don't get carried away by distracting thoughts. Attending to these mental markers at regular intervals in the course of the respiration is like taking note of milestones on the side of a country road, letting you know by their presence that you are on the right track, or by their absence that you have wandered off your chosen route.

This phase of the practice is primarily concerned with *mindfulness of breathing*, not *counting*. It's easy to maintain just enough continuity of attention to keep track of counting, while between counts, the mind wanders off on its own, like a dog without a leash. Let the counting remind you to keep your attention focused on the tactile sensations of the breath, which change from moment to moment. After counting the breath at the beginning of the inhalation, let your mind be as conceptually silent as possible for the remainder of the in-breath. And during the out-breath, release any involuntary thoughts that have cropped up. As mentioned before, arouse your attention (counteracting laxity) during the in-breath, and relax your attention (counteracting excitation) with each out-breath. But don't relax so much that you become spaced out or dull. In this way, with each complete breath, you remedy the two major defects of attention.

Meditation is a balancing act between attention and relaxation. Mastering this requires working to counter the natural reflex of trying harder, or clamping down, when you see that your mind has become distracted. Instead, as soon as you see that your mind has wandered, release the effort of clinging to the distracting thought or physical sensation, return to the breath, and relax more deeply. Remember that the main point of such attentional training is not to stop thoughts from arising. Rather, it is first to relax the body and mind, then to cultivate the stability of sustaining attention continuously upon your chosen object. Thoughts are bound to arise. Simply do your best not to be carried away by them.

The kind of awareness cultivated here is called *bare attention*, in which the mind is fully focused on the sensory impressions appearing to it, moment to moment, rather than getting caught up in conceptual and emotional responses to those stimuli. As you attend to the abdominal sensations of breathing, mental images of your body, based on visual memory, are likely to arise together with the bodily sensations themselves. Recognize the difference between the tactile sensations of the breath as they appear to bare attention, as opposed to the mental images of what you think your body looks like, which are superimposed by your conceptual mind. As soon as you note the presence of these mental images, release them and direct your attention solely to the immediate, tactile experiences of breathing.

Continue practicing for one twenty-four-minute period, experimenting with the counting. Sometimes try counting the breaths only toward the beginning of the session, sometimes throughout the whole session, and on other occasions count only intermittently when the mind especially gets caught up in conceptualization.

REFLECTIONS ON THE PRACTICE

We began this practice at stage one with a primary emphasis on relaxation. Generally, the more relaxed we are, the more stable our attention can become. But that relaxation must be balanced with vigilance, otherwise it will simply lead to laxity, sluggishness, or unbridled daydreaming. Once we have established a foundation of relaxation, we can more strongly emphasize attentional stability.

One way to cultivate attentional stability is to direct our attention downward to the sensations in the abdomen associated with the in- and out-breath. Mindfulness of the entire body is very helpful for relaxing the mind, but this technique of focusing on the abdomen, which is commonly taught in the Burmese Theravada tradition, can be especially helpful for stabilizing the mind.

Many Buddhist traditions, including Zen and Theravada Buddhism, encourage the practice of counting breaths as a means of stabilizing attention, and this advice is found in the Indian Mahayana tradition as well.

The *Theravada* Buddhist tradition is based on the teachings attributed to the Buddha as first recorded in the Pali language, and it is focused on the attainment of one's own individual liberation, or nirvana. The *Mahayana* tradition is based on the teachings attributed to the Buddha as recorded in Sanskrit, and it centers on the realization of buddhahood for the sake of all beings. One Mahayana sutra, for instance, states, "How do you correctly note, with the power of mindfulness, the in-and-out movement of the breath? You count them correctly."[13] Following the classic treatise *The Path of Purification*, a contemporary Sri Lankan scholar suggests counting from one to ten, with one count for each full respiration. After you get the hang of that, he says, you may progress to this more advanced technique:[14]

> The meditator, taking either inhalation or exhalation as his start-
> ing point, as he thinks fit, should begin counting "one" and repeat
> it until the next breath comes, as "one, one," "two, two," and thus
> up to "ten, ten," noting the breaths as they arise in succession. As
> he counts thus, the incoming breath and the outgoing breath
> become clear and distinct to his mind.

Asanga suggested an alternate technique:[15]

> When the inhalation has come in, count "one" with mindfulness
> applied to inhalation and exhalation. When the inhalation has
> ceased and the exhalation has gone out, count "two," counting
> thus up to ten. The number of the counting must not be too lit-
> tle or too much. This is called counting individually.

Buddhadasa, a twentieth-century Thai teacher, translated the word *ana-panasati*, which is usually translated as "mindfulness *of* breathing," as "mind-fulness *with* breathing."[16] What we attend *to* in this practice is the field of tactile sensations; what we attend *with* is the breathing. Do your best not to lose contact with the ebb and flow of the breath as it influences sensations in your abdomen. Keep your mind open and relaxed, never constricted.

You might be surprised to see how much discomfort arises in your body, even when your practice sessions are relatively short and your meditation cushion is comfortable. This is normal, so don't become discouraged. You may view involuntary thoughts and bodily tension as informative signs of underlying mental and physical imbalances and learn from them. The unrest you experience in your body and mind is not the real problem, it is symptomatic of the extent to which your whole psychosomatic system is out of tune. Let these symptoms remind you to relax the mind and breathe into areas of tension in the body.

AN ATTENTIVE WAY OF LIFE

Have you ever driven down a highway and let miles slip by without any recollection of where you've been or of anything else that was happening in that interval? Or have you ever been in a conversation with someone, only to find that you don't have a clue about what they've been saying for the past couple of minutes? These are just two common examples that may indicate a *cognitive deficit disorder*. When we succumb to such a mental imbalance, the mind goes absent without leave, and we wake up to our mindlessness only after the fact. The more we practice mindlessness, the better we get at it—there's no better way to kill time. Our lives just pass on by, without our noticing it. Psychiatric hospitals take care of people with disabling cases of mindlessness, but cognitive deficit disorders are common in society at large, and they are disabling for all of us.

Let's look at another kind of cognitive imbalance. Have your ever seen something that simply wasn't there, or heard someone make a remark that never left their lips? These are instances of a *cognitive hyperactivity disorder*, in which we project things onto the world, then assume that our projections are really out there. We all have this tendency, not just the mentally ill, and whenever we make such false superimpositions, this creates problems. Our experience of reality is out of kilter with what's going on around us, and when we behave as if our cognitively imbalanced experience is valid, we collide with reality. This is a source of unnecessary suffering.

Cognitive imbalances of both types can be remedied by applying to daily life the attention skills we cultivate during meditation. In fact, if we casually let our minds succumb to excitation and laxity throughout the day, there's little chance that our formal training during twenty-four-minute sessions is going to have much effect. This would be like eating a wholesome breakfast, then snacking on junk food for the rest of the day.

However busy we may be, or think we are, no one is paying us enough to have demands on our minds every single moment of the day. Even in the midst of work, we can take off fifteen seconds here and sixty seconds there to balance the attention by quietly focusing on the breath. Our eyes can be open, and we can sit quietly for a few moments, without calling attention to ourselves. We can do this in the workplace, while standing in line at the grocery store, or while waiting at a stoplight. There are many brief occasions from the time we get up in the morning until we fall asleep at night when we can "season our day" with a sprinkling of mindfulness of breathing. And each time we do it, we may immediately feel the soothing effect on our bodies and minds. In this way, we can begin to integrate the quality of awareness that we cultivate during meditation with the awareness that we bring to our activities in the world throughout the day.

The quality of bare attention we cultivate during mindfulness of the sensations of breathing can be applied to other sensations as well. The next time you sit down for a meal, try this experiment, in which you focus bare attention on each of your five physical senses as they arise in relation to the meal set before you. Let your visual, olfactory, gustatory, auditory, and tactile senses individually experience the food by way of bare attention, with as little conceptual overlay as possible.

Begin by directing your mindfulness to the visual appearance of the food—just its colors and shapes. Let go of any conceptual associations you may have regarding these visual impressions. Let go of preferences or judgments of the food. Your likes and dislikes are not present in the food itself, nor in its colors and shapes. Just be present with the shapes and colors of your meal, focusing on them with bare attention.

Now close your eyes for a few moments and focus on the smells of the food. Be totally present with just those fragrances, noting how they change from moment to moment. Recognize the nuances of these aromas with discerning mindfulness, but without mixing your immediate experience with labels and concepts, likes and dislikes. Now take a mouthful of the food and, with your eyes remaining closed, direct your bare attention to the tastes that arise in your mouth. Eat slowly, mindful of the changes in flavors that rise up to meet you. As you chew the food, direct your attention to the sounds of eating. They are never the same from moment to moment, so ride the crest of the wave of the present, clinging to nothing in the past, anticipating nothing in the future. Finally, apply bare attention to the tactile sensations of the food—its warmth or coldness, firmness or fluidity, smoothness or roughness. Release any mental images of what you think the food looks like, and focus solely on the tactile qualities of the food as it is chewed and swallowed.

Wasn't that interesting? Normally when we eat, especially if we are simultaneously involved in some other activity, such as engaging in a conversation, our conceptual overlays drown out the sensory qualities of the food we're eating. We remember only that we liked, disliked, or were indifferent to the meal, but we commonly suffer from a cognitive deficit disorder when it comes to the five kinds of sensory impressions we were receiving from the food. Just as a meal can pass by unnoticed, so can the rest of our lives. All too often, we miss out on what was happening, imagine things that never happened at all, and recall only the assumptions, expectations, and fantasies that we projected onto reality.

We can apply such bare attention at any time, taking the "fresh produce" of the world straight from the fields of the senses, without prepackaging raw experience with our old, habitual conceptual wrappings. The challenge here is to distinguish what reality is presenting to our senses from moment to moment from what we are superimposing on the world, often unconsciously. This is what the Buddha was referring to when he declared, "In the seen there is only the seen; in the heard, there is only the heard; in the sensed, there is only the sensed; in the mentally perceived, there is only the mentally perceived."[17]

According to Buddhist psychology, in any single moment of awareness, which may be as brief as one millisecond, attention is focused in only one sense field. But during the course of these momentary pulses of consciousness, attention jumps rapidly from one sense field to another, like a chimpanzee on amphetamines. In the blur of these shifts among the sense fields, the mind "makes sense" of the world by superimposing familiar conceptual grids on our perceptions. In this way our experience of the world is structured and appears familiar to us. This is not a bad thing. In fact, it would be very difficult to function in daily life without such conceptual structuring. But problems emerge when we fail to recognize the degree to which we are conceptually adding to reality or subtracting from it through sheer mindlessness. That's where the cognitive hyperactivity and deficit problems arise.

If this theory is valid (and cognitive scientists are exploring these issues today), then from moment to moment there's really no such thing as mental multitasking. At any given moment, our minds are on one thing only. So the experience of attending to multiple things at once is an illusion. What's really happening is that the attention is rapidly moving back and forth from one field of experience to another. Recent scientific research indicates that multitasking is in fact not very efficient, for the quality of awareness allotted to each task is diminished. It's as if we have a finite quantity of attention—like a finite volume of water flowing down a gorge—and as we direct it into smaller tributaries of interest, there's less attention available for each channel.

The practice of focused attention is essentially "non-multitasking." It's learning how to channel the stream of awareness where we wish, for as long as we wish, without it compulsively becoming fragmented and thrown into disarray. So when you are next confronted with the choice of whether to focus on a single experience at one time, or to divide your attention, consider your priorities. If something's worth doing, it's worth doing well, and if something's not worth doing, it's not worth doing at all. Even when we think we are multitasking, according to Buddhist psychology, we're actually moving our attention from one task to another with great rapidity. This is necessary at times, and when it is, try to do so as mindfully as possible.

INTERLUDE COMPASSION

When you start to experience the inner calm, simplicity, and quietude of shamatha practice, you may become attached to this state of mind, and that can result in apathetic indifference to those around you and the world at large. You've got your own quiet space of serenity, and you may not want to be disturbed. The worthy venture of meditative training becomes derailed when it results in such complacency; it can become little more than a substitute for Prozac or Valium. The real aim of this practice is to cultivate mental balance that results in genuine happiness, and indifference to others is not a sign of genuine happiness or mental health.

While some people become attached to the feelings of calm they experience through shamatha practice, others may become dissatisfied with their progress and become bored with the practice. This training usually does not provide swift gratification or immediate results. It can lead to exceptional mental health and well-being, but this takes time and effort.

Rather than suppressing the symptoms of an imbalanced mind by losing ourselves in work or entertainment, we can engage in our practice and go to the root of the problem and cultivate our minds. The word *meditation* in the modern world often has the connotation of doing something special to calm the mind or try to achieve some altered state of consciousness. But the Sanskrit word for meditation is *bhavana,* which simply means "cultivation." In fact, we are all cultivating our minds in one way or another all the time, through the way we use our attention. The quality of our lives reflects the ways we have cultivated our minds until now.

Impediment to mental balance that are especially common in the West
are self-judgment, guilt, and low self-esteem. As we practice, we may do so
with a certain level of expectation. Then, if we don't progress as well as we
think we should, we may grow impatient with ourselves and feel guilty
when we don't take time to practice. One more failure to add to our list! In
attentional training, we are going against the grain of years of habit, let
alone eons of biological evolution that have helped us survive and procre-
ate but have done little to prepare us for such serene, focused attention. So
it's no wonder that our minds are so scattered and prone to imbalances of
all kinds. But with gentle patience, we can gradually train our minds so that
they provide us with an inner sense of well-being, instead of constant anxiety, dissatisfaction, and restlessness. This requires compassion for ourselves
and for others.

The first step is to begin identifying the real causes of our discontent.
Virtually anything may catalyze unhappiness, but its true source is always
in the mind. Some people feel desperately miserable even when their
outer circumstances are wonderful, while others are happy and contented
even in the face of dire adversity. We suffer because our minds are
afflicted by various kinds of imbalances, which lead us to seek happiness
in all the wrong places. But we can emerge from this hedonic treadmill by
identifying what truly ails us and what truly brings us satisfaction.
Buddhists refer to this shift in priorities as the arousal of a *spirit of emergence*,
with which we move away from the sources of discontent and set out on
the path to genuine happiness. This is the most compassionate thing we
can do for ourselves.

None of us lives in isolation, no matter how lonely or alienated we may
feel at times. Our welfare is intimately linked to everyone around us, especially those with whom we are in frequent contact. As we learn to be compassionate and nonjudgmental toward ourselves, it is only natural to extend
this gentle heart to others. This begins with empathy—*feeling with* the joys
and sorrows, successes and failures of our loved ones, associates, and even
strangers. This is the fertile ground from which the seed of compassion
sprouts. But empathy and compassion are not the same. Compassion is not
simply feeling sorry for someone. Compassion goes beyond empathy to

the heartfelt yearning, "May you be free of suffering and its causes. How may I help?"

MEDITATION ON COMPASSION

Settle your body in its rest state, as described previously, and calm the mind for a few moments with mindfulness of breathing. Begin this session by cultivating compassion for yourself. How long have you struggled to free yourself of anxiety and dissatisfaction? What tendencies of your own mind and behavior have repeatedly gotten in your way? This is not a time for self-judgment, dismay, or apathy. It's a time for reappraisal. How can we free ourselves of the *inner* causes of suffering, given that we have so little control over *outer* circumstances? Let the aspiration arise: May I be free of the true causes of worry and sadness. Envision your mind free of pointless cravings, free of hostility, and free of confusion. Imagine the serenity and joy of a balanced mind, closely in tune with reality.

Now direct your attention to a loved one who is suffering from physical or psychological distress. The very term *attention* is related to the verb "to tend," as in "to take care of" and "to watch over." When you attend to someone fully, you are offering yourself to her. This is your most intimate gift—to attend to someone with a loving, compassionate heart. Let this person fill your heart and mind. Attend to this person's experience, and if you know the causes of her grief or pain, be present with those causes. Imagine shifting your attention into her perspective, experiencing her difficulties. Then return to your own perspective and let the yearning arise, "May you be free from suffering and the causes of suffering." Imagine this person finding relief and the freedom that she seeks to lead a happy and meaningful life.

Bring to mind another person, one who wishes to be free of suffering but out of delusion causes his own and others' suffering. Again, imagine taking his perspective and experiencing his difficulties. Then, return to your own perspective, and with an understanding of the consequences of this person's behavior, wish that he be free of the mental afflictions at the root of his destructive behavior. Let the heartfelt wish arise, "May you have a clear vision of the path to freedom from suffering," and imagine this person free of the causes of suffering.

Now let the scope of your awareness rove through the world, attending to those who suffer, whether from hunger and thirst, from poverty or the miseries of war, from social injustice or the imbalances and afflictions of their own minds. We are all deserving of compassion, especially when we act out of delusion, harming ourselves and others. Let your heart embrace the world with the aspiration, "May we all be free of suffering and its true causes. May we all help ease each others' pain."[18]

STAGE 3: RESURGENT ATTENTION ● ● ●

When you reach the third stage, *resurgent attention*, during each practice session your attention is fixed most of the time upon your meditative object. By now, you will have increased the duration of each session beyond the initial twenty-four minutes to perhaps twice that. As your attention gradually stabilizes, you may increase the duration of each session by increments of three minutes. At all times, though, value the *quality* of your meditation over the *quantity* of time spent in each session. If you sit for long periods but let your mind rove around unnoticed among distractions or fall into dullness, not only are you wasting your time, but also you are developing bad habits that will only get harder and harder to break.

When you were still on the second stage, although you experienced periods when your attention was continually engaged with the meditative object for as long as a minute, most of the time you were still caught up in distractions. When you reach the third stage, your attentional stability has increased so that most of the time you remain engaged with the object. Occasionally there are still lapses when you completely forget the object, but you quickly recognize them and patch up these holes in the continuity of attention. Long before you achieve this stage, you may occasionally have a session in which your mind seems to remain on the object most of the time. But don't be fooled! Even amateur golfers occasionally hit a birdie, but that doesn't mean they're ready to go on the pro circuit. The third stage is achieved only when your mind remains focused on the object most of the time in virtually all your sessions. For most people, the primary problem in this phase of practice is still coarse excitation, and it is with the power of mindfulness that you accomplish this third stage.

From the beginning of shamatha training, however, some people are more prone to laxity, which manifests in coarse, medium, and subtle degrees. For the moment, we'll concern ourselves only with *coarse laxity*, which occurs when your attention mostly disengages from the object and sinks into a spaced-out vacancy. This is like having the reception of a radio station mostly fade out, even without interference from another channel. Abiding in a state of coarse laxity can be very peaceful, with your mind relatively undisturbed by thoughts or emotional upheavals. But if you spend many hours each day in such a state of dullness, Tibetan contemplatives report that this not only has no benefit, it can actually impair your intelligence. The acuity of your mind starts to atrophy, and over the long term, this can do serious damage. During the early 1970s, I knew of one fellow who decided on his own that the whole point of meditation was to stop thinking, and he diligently applied himself to this goal for days on end. Eventually, he reached this goal by becoming vegetative, unable even to feed himself, and he needed to be hospitalized. This might be deemed an extreme case of coarse laxity!

As you continue in this practice, in order to progress through the stages of attentional development, you need to hone the ability to monitor the quality of your attention. While the main force of your awareness is directed to the meditation object with *mindfulness*, this needs to be supported with the faculty of *introspection*, which allows for the quality control of attention, enabling you to swiftly note when the mind has fallen into either excitation or laxity. As soon as you detect either imbalance, take the necessary steps to remedy it. Your first antidote to excitation is to relax more deeply; to counteract laxity, arouse your attention.

Throughout all the first three stages, involuntary thoughts flow like a cascading waterfall. But over time, these currents of compulsive ideation carry you away less and less frequently. Coarse excitation gradually subsides, even though thoughts and mental images continue to crop up, as do sounds, smells, and other sensory appearances. Don't try to block out these distractions. Simply let them go and refocus your attention as single-pointedly as you can on your chosen object of meditation.

Many people appear to achieve the second stage while meditating just one or two sessions each day. In their more focused sessions, they experience periods of continuity of attention, but such stability is lost during the day as they engage in other activities. Shamatha meditation can be very helpful even in the midst of a normal, socially active way of life, especially when it is balanced with other kinds of spiritual practice, such as the cultivation of loving-kindness and compassion. Rounded, integrated practice is like maintaining a healthy diet. While a proper diet won't necessarily heal imbalance and illness, it is still indispensable for maintaining your vitality and resistance to disease. Likewise, a balanced meditative practice in the course of a socially engaged way of life heightens your psychological immune system, so that you are less vulnerable to mental imbalances of all kinds.

If you are practicing for only a session or two each day, you may not progress beyond the second attentional stage. The reason for this is simple: if you are balancing your attention for an hour or so each day, but letting it become fragmented and distracted for the other fifteen hours of waking time each day, then the attentional coherence cultivated during these brief sessions is overwhelmed by the distractions of the rest of the day. The achievement of the stage of resurgent attention requires a greater commitment to practice. This will entail multiple sessions of meditation each day, practiced within a quiet, contemplative way of life that supports the cultivation of inner calm and collectedness. The key to success is to conduct your life between sessions in such a way that you don't lose the ground you have gained.

THE PRACTICE:
MINDFULNESS OF BREATHING WITH VIVIDNESS

Begin this twenty-four-minute session, as always, by settling your body in its rest state, imbued with the three qualities of relaxation, stillness, and vigilance. Take three slow, deep breaths, breathing down into the abdomen and then into the chest. Let your awareness permeate your body, feeling the sensations of the respiration wherever they arise. Then let your breath flow of its own accord, settling into its natural rhythm.

Mentally, the initial emphasis in shamatha practice is on relaxation, which can be induced by attending to the sensations of breathing throughout the body. The second emphasis is on stability of attention, and for this it can be helpful to observe the sensations of breathing in the region of the belly. Then, having established a foundation of relaxation and stability, we shift the emphasis to cultivating vividness of attention. It is crucially important that stability is not gained at the expense of relaxation, and that the increase of vividness does not coincide with the decrease of stability. The relationship among these three qualities can be likened to the roots, trunk, and foliage of a tree. As your practice grows, the roots of relaxation go deeper, the trunk of stability gets stronger, and the foliage of vividness reaches higher.

In this practice session, shift the emphasis to vividness. You do this by elevating the focus of attention and directing it to a subtler object. Direct your attention to the tactile sensations of your breath at the apertures of your nostrils or above your upper lip, wherever you feel the in- and out-flow of your breath. Elevating the focus of attention helps to induce vividness, and attending to a subtle object enhances that further. Observe these sensations at the gateway of the respiration, even between breaths. There is an ongoing flow of tactile sensations in the area of the nostrils and upper lip, so sustain your attention there as continuously as possible. If the breath becomes so subtle that you can't detect the sensations of its flow, quiet your mind and observe more carefully. As you arouse the vividness of attention, eventually the sensations of the breath will become evident again.

On the periphery of your awareness, you may still note other sensations throughout your body, as well as sounds and so on. Just let them be, without trying to block them out, and focus your attention single-pointedly on the sensations around the apertures of your nostrils.

Count your breaths if you find this helpful. Arouse your faculty of introspection so that you quickly note whether excitation or laxity has arisen, and take the necessary steps to balance the attention when such problems occur. Continue practicing for one twenty-four-minute period, then bring the session to a close.

REFLECTIONS ON THE PRACTICE

The Buddha described the practice of mindfulness of breathing with the following analogy:

> Just as in the last month of the hot season, when a mass of dust and dirt has swirled up, a great rain cloud out of season disperses it and quells it on the spot, so too concentration by mindfulness of breathing, when developed and cultivated, is peaceful and sublime, an ambrosial dwelling, and it disperses and quells on the spot unwholesome states whenever they arise.[19]

This analogy refers to the healing effect of balanced attention. When awareness is brought to rest on a neutral object, such as the breath, immediately every distressing thought disappears, and the mind becomes peaceful, sublime, and happy. These qualities do not arise from the object of awareness—the breath—but from the nature of the mind in a state of balance. This approach to healing the mind is similar to healing the physical body. The Buddha implied in his rain cloud analogy that the mind, like the body, has an innate power to heal itself. By clearly attending to a neutral object with sustained attention, without craving or aversion, we enable the mind to begin its own healing.

Since coarse excitation is still the predominant problem during the third stage of attentional development, you may find it helpful to continue counting the breaths. Some Theravada teachers, following the fifth-century scholar Buddhaghosa, offer two methods involving "quick counting." In the first of these techniques, you count from one to ten with each full respiration. In the second, with each full breath cycle you count, "one, two, three, four, five; one, two, three, four, five, six; one, two, three, four, five, six, seven; ...eight; ...nine; ...ten."[20] Asanga, on the other hand, suggested counting the breaths backward, from ten to one. After that, you may try counting two breaths as one, four as one, and so on, slowing the pace of counting to include ever larger clusters of breaths. However you choose to count the breaths, when your attention stabilizes to such an extent that you no longer experience lapses of attention but remain continuously engaged with each inhalation and exhalation, you can stop counting. That temporary crutch has served its purpose. Asanga commented, though, that the various methods for counting the breaths are not for everyone. They may help some people to counteract laxity and excitation, but others may find that they can focus their attention quite effectively on the respiration without counting. Such people don't need to bother with any of the above counting techniques.

As your mind calms, you may find that your respiration becomes subtler, and this results in fainter sensations of breathing. The further you progress in this practice, the subtler the breath becomes. At times it may become so subtle that you can't detect it at all. This challenges you to enhance the vividness of attention. In other words, you have to pay closer and closer attention to these sensations in order to stay mentally engaged with the breath.[21] There's a kind of biofeedback process at work here. If your mind becomes distracted and you get caught up in involuntary thoughts, your breathing will become coarser, resulting in stronger sensations, which are easier to detect. But as your mind calms down again, the breathing and the sensations that go with it become finer, and this once again challenges you to heighten the degree of vividness. Mindfulness of breathing has this unique "biofeedback" advantage.

Various physical sensations may occur in meditation. Sometimes you may feel that your limbs are extremely heavy or thick. Sometimes your body may feel very large. Or you may feel that you are floating or levitating. Other sensations such as tingling, vibration, or heat are common. You may experience telescopic vision, viewing your body as if from a distance. Especially when you meditate many hours a day, you may experience within your body *prana*, or vital energies, shifting and releasing pockets of tension. When you engage in mindfulness of breathing, these energies begin to balance and flow naturally. This is a process that takes time, and while the energies redistribute themselves, their movement produces various sensations. Don't be worried about them or make a big deal of them; these are natural consequences of the practice.

The practice of shamatha results in an anomalous kind of attention. Normally, when the mind is relaxed, attention is slack, and when attention is aroused, this brings with it a state of tension, a tightening of the body and mind. But in this practice, the more you arouse your attention, the more deeply the mind relaxes. There's a relatively egoless quality to shamatha; while other activities that call for a high level of concentration are effortful and often goal oriented, shamatha entails doing almost nothing. You're passively attending to the sensations of the breath without regulating it in any way. Your ego is mostly taken out of commission as you let the body breathe of its own accord, exerting only a subtle degree of effort to balance attention when it falls into laxity or excitation.

As you advance in the practice, increase the duration of each meditation session and decrease the number of sessions each day. Always go for quality over quantity.

Unbroken continuity of practice is vital. Imagine starting a fire by rubbing two sticks together: if you rub the sticks together for only a few moments, then rest, then do it for a few moments, then rest, you could continue in this way for years without even igniting a spark. Likewise, if you are intent on progressing through all the nine stages, the time-tested way to proceed is to radically simplify your life, withdraw temporarily into solitude, and devote yourself full-time to this practice for extended periods. It is not easy to achieve the bliss of shamatha without leaving heavily populated areas, which tend to be noisy and congested. In contrast, in the wilderness, removed from society, a meditator can more easily set his mind at ease and accomplish meditative stabilization.

AN ATTENTIVE WAY OF LIFE

The major challenge at this stage of the practice is to adopt a lifestyle that supports the cultivation of attentional balance, rather than eroding it between sessions. To achieve stage three, the dedicated meditator will need to take up this practice as a serious avocation, spending days or weeks in this practice in the midst of a contemplative way of life in a serene, quiet environment. If we practice only a session or two each day while leading an active life, we may occasionally feel that we've reached the sustained attention of the third stage, but we'll have a hard time stabilizing at that level. The busy-ness of the day intrudes, the mind becomes scattered, and the attentional coherence gained during meditation will likely be lost.

The modern world constantly reminds us that we are "social creatures" and provides little incentive or encouragement to spend long periods in solitude. Many people even think that extended solitary meditation is anti-social, or is a behavior associated with mental deviants rather than with people striving to achieve exceptional mental balance. Solitude and seclusion are associated for many with boredom, loneliness, fear, and depression. It's no wonder that penal systems around the world use solitary confinement to punish unruly prisoners. But why do people so often find solitude and inactivity distressing? In the absence of distractions, we come face to face with our own minds, and if they are seriously imbalanced, we relentlessly experience the symptoms of these mental afflictions with no buffer zone, no distractions, and no escape.

While the value of solitude is often lost on the public today, there have always been proponents of simplicity of lifestyle so that we can devote ourselves to quiet contemplation. Henry David Thoreau explained why he withdrew into solitude by Walden Pond: "I went to the woods because I wished to live deliberately, to front only the essential facts of life, and see if I could not learn what it had to teach, and not, when I came to die, discover that I had not lived."[22] Solitary meditation doesn't *cause* mental imbalances, but *uncovers* them. Boredom may set in, especially when the mind succumbs to laxity, and restlessness often comes in the wake of excitation. With perseverance you can move beyond these imbalances and begin to discover the well-being that arises from a balanced mind. But this requires courage to face your own inner demons and persist in the practice despite the emotional upheavals that are bound to occur in the course of this training.

PREPARING FOR AN EXPEDITION

When I lead shamatha seminars, I like to think of them as "expeditions" rather than "retreats." The word "retreat" has the connotation not only of withdrawal but also of defeat, and that certainly isn't the spirit of such practice. The word "expedition," on the other hand, suggests adventure, conquest, and exploration. The Latin roots of the word have to do with extricating yourself, literally "stepping out," of some situation in which you've gotten stuck. In the practice of shamatha, we discover how deeply our minds are trapped in the twin ruts of excitation and laxity. In the Buddhist tradition, a mind trapped in these ruts is said to be dysfunctional, and in order to make it serviceable, it is helpful to step out of our normal activities, seek out a spacious sense of solitude, and explore the frontiers of the mind.

This expedition doesn't require blind faith or allegiance to any religious creed or metaphysical belief system. Over the past three millennia, contemplatives from various Asian cultures, with diverse belief systems, have followed the path of shamatha to its culmination, and they have reported their findings. We don't need to accept their claims simply on their own authority, but if we are inspired by earlier accounts of the benefits of this practice, we may venture forth on this path to see for ourselves whether we can achieve the results of the contemplative explorers who have preceded us.

There are great adventures ahead, but also perils and dead ends. Sometimes the path is clear, but now and then it may seem to disappear altogether. The purpose of relying on those who know this path from their own experience is to save time.

Six prerequisites for sustained, rigorous training are set forth in many Indian and Tibetan Buddhist meditation manuals.[23] These are some of the essential causes and conditions that will produce the fruit of shamatha.

1. A Supportive Environment

It's important to practice in a safe, quiet, and agreeable location, optimally with a few other like-minded people. This should be a place where food, clothing, and other necessities are easily obtained. Finding such an environment sounds simple in principle, but in practice it can be very difficult, especially if you try to devote yourself to practice for months on end.

I discovered this through my own experience back in 1980. I'd moved into a cabin in India to engage in solitary meditation. From the outside, the site looked idyllic. Perched on a rocky mountain ledge in northern India, it overlooked the verdant Kangra Valley to the south and the ramparts of the Himalayas to the north.

It was a blessing to live there, but I also had to deal with legions of bed-bugs who invaded my sleeping bag every night and even crept into my robes to drink my blood during the day while I sat in meditation. Even if I caught them, as a Buddhist monk I wouldn't kill them. Every morning, around two o'clock, I would wake up with my skin marked with welts that itched like a hundred mosquito bites. I would collect the critters in a metallic mug from which they couldn't escape, and in the morning I would throw the night's catch over the side of the mountain. They would then climb back up and prepare for the next night's invasion. This went on for two months before I discovered that I could keep them out of my sleeping bag by laying it on a raised platform with each of its legs inserted inside a can filled with water. Though I succeeded in warding off the bedbug invasions, I still had to deal with the fleas, mosquitoes, and rats, as well as the penetrating mildew that set in shortly after the monsoon began.

After four years of meditation, two in Asia and two in North America, I concluded that—unless you're wealthy and can simply purchase a place to meditate in quiet for months or years on end—a suitable environment is hard to come by. Nevertheless, it's necessary to create such places if people in the modern world wish to progress very far along the path of shamatha.

2 & 3. Having Few Desires and Being Content

The first of these two prerequisites refers to having few desires for things you *don't* have, and the second refers to being content with what you *do* have. Without these two qualities, your mind will never settle down in the practice. You will be constantly thinking of things you want but don't have, and you will fret that your present circumstances are inadequate in one way or another. This does not mean that you must quell your desire for happiness, but it is necessary to refocus your aspirations on transforming your own mind as the means to genuine well-being. And for this to happen, you must see the limitations of a life driven by such mundane pursuits as wealth, luxury, entertainment, and reputation. All these circumstances can give you is a temporary spurt of pleasure that tapers off as soon as the pleasurable stimulus stops. Mental balance is the gateway to finding genuine happiness, and shamatha is the key that opens that gate.

The Buddha illustrated this point with the story of an elephant that entered a shallow pond to refresh itself on a hot summer day.[24] Given its great size, the elephant could find a footing in the deep water and enjoy itself. Then a cat came along and, wishing to escape the heat of the day, jumped into the same pond. But unlike the elephant, the cat couldn't find any footing, so it had only two options: either to sink to the bottom or float to the top. Similarly, those who have accustomed themselves to having few desires and contentment can find joy in solitude, whereas those who have not found such equilibrium are bound either to sink into laxity and depression or to float up into excitation and restlessness.

4. Having Few Activities

While you are devoting yourself to shamatha training, it is important to keep other activities to a minimum, for if your behavior between meditation sessions erodes the coherence of attention that you gained during sessions, then you won't be able to gain any ground. Given the fast pace of modern life and the general emphasis on keeping busy, it can be difficult to make this shift to simplicity. Our work can be a kind of narcotic, concealing the unrest and turbulence of our minds. And a lifestyle that alternates between hard work and hard play can keep us constantly busy, without ever gaining a clue about the meaning of life or the potentials of human consciousness.

5. Ethical Discipline

A necessary foundation for balancing the mind is ethical discipline, which is far more than merely following social rules or religious commandments from an external source of authority. To live harmoniously with others, we need to practice social ethics, and to live harmoniously within our natural environment, we need to practice environmental ethics. The practice of ethics involves avoiding harm to others by means of our physical, verbal, or mental behavior, and leads to social and environmental flourishing, in which whole communities may live in harmony with each other and with their natural environment.[25]

A third type of ethical discipline is psychophysical ethics. To promote inner well-being, we need to practice ethical ways of treating our own bodies and minds. This includes taking good care of the body, following a healthy diet, and getting the right kind and amount of physical exercise. It also involves engaging in mental behavior that is conducive to balancing the mind and reducing disturbing mental states such as hatred, greed, confusion, fear, and jealousy.

The call to ethical discipline challenges each of us to examine our own behavior carefully, noting both short-term and long-term consequences of our actions. Although an activity may yield immediate pleasure, if over time it results in unrest, conflict, and misery, it warrants the label "unwholesome." On the other hand, while a behavior may involve difficulties in the short-term, we can regard it as "wholesome" if it eventually leads to contentment, harmony, and genuine happiness for ourselves and others.

Environmental, social, and psychophysical ethics all involve living in ways that are conducive to our own and others' well-being. An ethical way of life supports the cultivation of mental balance, and this in turn further enables us to promote our own and others' well-being.

6. Dispensing with Compulsive Thoughts

Many of us let compulsive thoughts dominate our minds. These won't stop overnight, but as we engage in shamatha practice, both during and between sessions, it is important to observe the mind's activities and restrain it when it falls into thought patterns that aggravate mental disturbances. Otherwise, we'll be like the cat that thrashes around on the surface of the pond, never free from the turbulence of our own minds.

The Indian Buddhist sage Atisha wrote of the importance of these prerequisites:[26]

> As long as the prerequisites for shamatha
> Are incomplete, meditative stabilization
> Will not be accomplished, even if you meditate
> Strenuously for thousands of years.

In our material society, even for people who are drawn to nonmaterialistic values, there's a strong tendency to take our current way of life as the norm, and then to add meditation to fix it, like a Band-Aid applied to a festering wound. My first experience with meditation in the late 1960s is a good example. I went to a teacher who gave me a mantra and told me how to meditate on it, but in these instructions there was no reference to the way I should lead the rest of my life. Even now, decades later, meditation is often taught with little or no reference to any of the above prerequisites. It has been reduced to a kind of first aid to alleviate the symptoms of a dysfunctional life, with all its anxieties, depression, frustration, and emotional vacillations. For a mind that is assaulted with a myriad of mental afflictions such as craving, hostility, and delusion, we need more than a medic. We need long-term, intensive care. That's what this training is all about.

INTERLUDE EMPATHETIC JOY

W hen you enter a long meditation retreat, you may first experience a sense of relief to be away from your normal way of life, with all its demands and concerns. But after this "honeymoon" phase of the retreat is over, the hard work of training the mind begins. The lifestyle itself while in retreat can be quite a challenge. While living in society, you can easily take your mind off your mind by losing yourself in work, entertainment, conversation, and many other kinds of busy-ness. But in the simple, uncluttered lifestyle of a contemplative, you are removed from external sources of distraction, and the physical and mental reactions to this can be intense.

We are addicted to pleasurable stimuli, and when we devote ourselves many hours each day to shamatha training, with few distractions between sessions, we begin to have withdrawal symptoms. The mind oscillates between boredom and restlessness, and at times it may descend into depression and self-doubt. At such times, we tend to fixate on ideas and memories that reinforce such gloom and doom, so it's important to lift ourselves out of these emotional sinkholes by reflecting on other aspects of reality that inspire us. One such practice is the meditative cultivation of empathetic joy.

In the practice of loving-kindness and compassion, we cultivate a yearning that others may find happiness and its causes and be free from suffering and its causes. The cultivation of the empathetic joy involves attending closely to something that is already a reality—the joys, successes, and virtues of yourself and others. Empathy is *feeling with others,* and in this practice we focus not on their sorrows and difficulties, but on their happiness and triumphs. This practice is a direct antidote to feelings of depression, anxiety, and hopelessness that may arise in the course of intensive, sustained meditation, or simply in the course of daily living.

MEDITATION ON EMPATHETIC JOY

Find a comfortable position, keeping the spine straight. Settle your body in its rest state, imbued with the three qualities of relaxation, stillness, and vigilance. Bring to mind a person you know well who exudes a sense of good cheer and well-being. Think of this person's physical presence, words, and actions. As you attend to this person's joy, open your heart to that joy and take delight in it. This will be easy if you already feel close to this person.

Now, bring to mind another individual. Think of someone for whom something wonderful has happened, recently or in the past. Recall the delight of this person and share in the joy.

Now direct your attention to someone who inspires you with his or her virtues, such as generosity, kindness, and wisdom. Rejoice in these virtues for this person's sake, for your own sake, and for all those who are recipients of this virtue.

Now direct awareness to your own life. Empathetic joy in our own virtues is important yet often overlooked. Attend to periods in your life that have been a source of inspiration to you and perhaps to others as well. Think of occasions when you embodied your own ideals. Attend to and take delight in your own virtues. There doesn't need to be any pompousness here, or any sense of pride or arrogance. As you recall the people and circumstances that enabled you to live well and enjoy the sweet fruits of your efforts, you may simultaneously experience a deep sense of gratitude and joy. This prevents you from slipping into a superficial sense of self-congratulation and superiority.

Some practices are difficult, but the practice of empathetic joy is easy. Throughout the course of the day, when you see or hear about someone's virtue or good fortune, empathetically take joy in it. This will raise your own spirits and help you climb out of emotional sinkholes of depression and low self-esteem.

STAGE 4: CLOSE ATTENTION ● ● ●

By maintaining continuity of this training in a retreat setting, you will eventually achieve the fourth of the nine stages of attentional development, called *close attention*. At this point, due to the power of enhanced mindfulness, you no longer completely forget your chosen object, the tactile sensations of the breath at the nostrils. You may have experienced glimpses of this level of attentional stability intermittently before actually achieving this stage, but now it has become normal. Each of your sessions may now last an hour or longer, and throughout this time, your attention cannot be involuntarily drawn entirely away from the object. You are now free of coarse excitation. It's as if the attention has acquired a kind of gravity such that it can't be easily buffeted by gusts of involuntary thoughts and sensory distractions.

At this stage it is said that you achieve the *power of mindfulness*.[27] In the Indian and Tibetan Mahayana traditions, mindfulness is defined as the mental faculty of maintaining attention, without forgetfulness or distraction, on a familiar object. Since mindfulness prevents the attention from straying from one's chosen object, it acts as the basis for single-pointed, focused attention, known as *samadhi*.[28] Asanga defined mindfulness as "the nonforgetfulness of the mind with respect to a familiar object, having the function of nondistraction."[29] Likewise, his brother Vasubandhu defined it as not losing the object of the mind.[30]

In recent years, a growing number of psychologists have been conducting research on mindfulness and its relevance to stress reduction, depression, and the alleviation of many other physical and mental problems. But they have characterized it in ways that are very different from the above description. According to one psychological paper on this topic, mindfulness is "a kind of nonelaborative, nonjudgmental, present-centered awareness in which each thought, feeling, or sensation that arises in the attentional field is acknowledged and accepted as it is."[31] The authors of this paper propose a two-component model of mindfulness, the first involving the self-regulation of attention so that it is maintained on immediate experience, and the second involving an orientation that is characterized by curiosity, openness, and acceptance.

The modern psychological account of mindfulness, which is explicitly based on the descriptions of mindfulness presented in the modern Vipassana (contemplative insight) tradition of Theravada Buddhism, differs significantly from the Indo-Tibetan Buddhist version. The modern Vipassana approach views mindfulness as nondiscriminating, moment-to-moment "bare awareness"; the Indo-Tibetan tradition, however, characterizes mindfulness as bearing in mind the object of attention, the state of not forgetting, not being distracted, and not floating.[32]

The scholar and teacher Bhante Gunaratana gives a clear description of the Vipassana view of mindfulness in his book *Mindfulness in Plain English*. There he describes mindfulness as nonconceptual awareness, or "bare attention," which does not label or categorize experiences. "Mindfulness," he says, "is present-time awareness...It stays forever in the present...If you are remembering your second-grade teacher, that is memory. When you then become aware that you are remembering your second-grade teacher, that is mindfulness."[33]

While Gunaratana's description is representative of the current Vipassana tradition as a whole, it is oddly at variance with the Buddha's own description of mindfulness, or *sati*: "And what monks, is the faculty of sati? Here, monks, the noble disciple has sati, he is endowed with perfect sati and intellect, he is one who remembers, who recollects what was done and said long before."[34] In contrast to the Vipassana tradition's insistence that mindfulness stays forever in the present, the Buddha states that it recollects events that are long past. Indeed, it is well known that the Pali term *sati* has as its primary meaning "recollection," or "memory," which is a conceptual faculty with which we recall past events. In addition to its connotation of "retrospective memory," sati also refers to "prospective memory," which enables us to remember to do things in the present and future, and this requires that the mind engage with concepts.

The *Milindapanha* is possibly the earliest attempt in Buddhist literature to state fully just what sati is. Questioned by King Milinda about the characteristics of sati, the monk Nagasena replies that it has both the characteristic of "calling to mind" and the characteristic of "taking hold." He explained further,

> Sati, when it arises, calls to mind wholesome and unwholesome tendencies, with faults and faultless, inferior and refined, dark and pure, together with their counterparts.... Sati, when it arises, follows the courses of beneficial and unbeneficial tendencies: these tendencies are beneficial, these unbeneficial; these tendencies are helpful, these unhelpful.[35]

So, rather than refraining from labeling or categorizing experiences in a nonjudgmental fashion, in the earliest, most authoritative accounts, sati is said to distinguish between wholesome and unwholesome, beneficial and unbeneficial tendencies. The contrast between the ancient and modern accounts is striking.

With his usual meticulous care, Buddhaghosa, the most authoritative commentator of the Theravada tradition, wrote:

> [Sati's] characteristic is not floating; its property is not losing; its manifestation is guarding or the state of being face to face with an object; its basis is strong noting or the close applications of mindfulness of the body and so on. It should be seen as like a post due to its state of being set in the object, and as like a gatekeeper because it guards the gate of the eye and so on.[36]

The modern description and practice of mindfulness are certainly valuable, as thousands of people have discovered for themselves through their own practice. But this doesn't take away from the fact that the modern understanding departs significantly from the Buddha's own account of sati, and from those of the most authoritative commentators in the Theravada and Indian Mahayana traditions.

Mindfulness is *cultivated* in the practice of shamatha, and it is *applied* in the practice of contemplative insight (Pali: *vipassana;* Sanskrit: *vipashyana*). This is clearly illustrated in the most foundational of all the Buddha's presentations of the practice of contemplative insight, namely his discourse on the four applications of mindfulness.[37] In this matrix of insight practices, discerning mindfulness is directed to the body, feelings, mental states and processes, and phenomena at large. Here the Buddha guides one through a detailed investigation of the origination, presence, causal efficacy, and dissolution of each of these domains of experience. This constitutes a rigorous contemplative science of the mind and its relation to the body and the environment, so there is much more to this discipline than bare attention alone, as is made abundantly clear in Buddhaghosa's authoritative commentary on this subject.[38]

As mentioned previously, in the fourth stage of shamatha practice, you achieve the power of mindfulness, and the practice comes into its own. While your attention is no longer prone to coarse excitation, it is still flawed by a medium degree of excitation and coarse laxity.

When medium excitation occurs, you don't completely lose track of your object of attention, but involuntary thoughts occupy the center of attention and the meditative object is displaced to the periphery. To compare this with coarse excitation, let's again take the analogy of tuning into a radio station. Coarse excitation is like losing your chosen station altogether, as your tuner slips either to another station or into mere static. Medium excitation is like drifting slightly toward another station but not so completely that you can no longer hear your chosen station at all. You still hear it, but it's muffled by extraneous noise.

The achievement of the fourth stage brings with it a sense of accomplishment. You are now an experienced shamatha trainee, no longer a complete beginner. If you have not gained a sound conceptual understanding of the entire shamatha path, you might well think you have already come to its culmination. This can easily give rise to some degree of complacency concerning your meditative practice, which brings its own dangers.

THE PRACTICE:
MINDFULNESS OF BREATHING WITH THE ACQUIRED SIGN

After settling your body and respiration in their natural states, continue focusing your attention on the bare sensations of the breath at the apertures of your nostrils. At this stage in the practice, your respiration will be very calm and the tactile sensations of the breath will be correspondingly very subtle. They may even become so faint that you can't detect them at all. When that happens, it is important not to assume that there are no sensations, nor should you deliberately breathe more vigorously so that you can pick up those sensations again. Rather, observe more and more closely until you do detect the very subtle sensations of your breath.

As discussed previously, this is a unique quality of the breath as a meditation object. In other methods for developing shamatha, the object is bound to become more and more evident as you progress in the practice. But with the technique of mindfulness of breathing, as your practice deepens, the breath becomes more and more subtle, which challenges you to arouse greater and greater vividness of attention. So, rise to this challenge as you simultaneously cultivate a deeper sense of relaxation, stronger stability, and brighter vividness.

Allow your respiration, which represents the "air element" of lightness and movement, to carry the healing, balancing, soothing process deeper and deeper. Habitual mental images, arising involuntarily, will be superimposed on your sense impressions, including tactile sensations. In this practice, you are like a chemist separating out the impurities of superimpositions from the pure strain of the tactile sensations of the breath. As superimpositions are released, the sense of your body having definite physical borders fades and you enter deeper and deeper levels of tranquillity.

In the phases of mindfulness of breathing thus far, you have been attending in various ways to the tactile sensations of the respiration. However, to continue all the way along the path of shamatha, eventually you must shift your attention from the tactile sensations of breathing to an "acquired sign" (Pali: *uggaha-nimitta*), a symbol of the air element that appears before the mind's eye as you progress in shamatha practice. To different people, acquired signs associated with the breath practice may appear like a star, a cluster of gems or pearls, a wreath of flowers, a puff of smoke, a cobweb, a cloud, a lotus flower, a wheel, or the moon or sun. The various appearances of the acquired sign are related to the mental dispositions of individual meditators. If you wish to continue on the path of mindfulness of breathing—which here explicitly turns into "mindfulness *with* breathing"—as soon as such a sign arises, shift your attention to this sign. This will be your object of attention as you proceed along the rest of the nine stages leading to shamatha.

At first your sign will arise only sporadically, so when it disappears, return to the previous sensations of the breath. But eventually it will appear more regularly and steadily, and from that point onward, focus your attention on this object. As you progress in this practice, increase the duration of your sessions for as long as you are able to maintain a quality of attention relatively free of laxity and excitation.

REFLECTIONS ON THE PRACTICE

The more advanced phases of the shamatha practice of mindfulness of breathing involving the acquired sign are described most authoritatively in Buddhaghosa's classic volume *The Path of Purification*.[39] While Buddhaghosa includes certain kinds of tactile sensations among the acquired signs associated with the breath practice, the Indo-Tibetan Mahayana tradition emphasizes that advanced stages along the path to shamatha can be achieved only by focusing on a mental object, not a sensory impression.[40] The reason for this is that the development of shamatha entails the cultivation of an exceptionally high degree of attentional vividness. By focusing on an object of any of the physical senses, you can certainly develop stability, but vividness will not be enhanced to its full potential. For this, a mental object is needed. It is commonly pointed out in the Buddhist tradition that shamatha is achieved with mental awareness, not sensory awareness.

Practicing mindfulness of breathing has its roots in the Buddha's teachings as written down in the Pali language and later commented on by Theravada scholars and contemplatives, and discourses attributed to the Buddha in the Mahayana tradition also emphasize this way of developing attentional balance. In *The Perfection of Wisdom Sutra in Ten Thousand Stanzas*, for example, the Buddha describes mindfulness of breathing to his disciple Shariputra by way of an analogy of a potter at his wheel.

> Shariputra, take the analogy of a potter or a potter's apprentice spinning the potter's wheel: If he makes a long revolution, he knows it is long; if he makes a short revolution, he knows it is short. Shariputra, similarly, a Bodhisattva, a great being, mindfully breathes in and mindfully breathes out. If the inhalation is long, he knows the inhalation is long; if the exhalation is long, he knows the exhalation is long. If the inhalation is short, he knows the inhalation is short; if the exhalation is short, he knows the exhalation is short. Shariputra, thus, a Bodhisattva, a great being, by dwelling with introspection and with mindfulness, eliminates avarice and disappointment towards the world by means of nonobjectification; and he lives observing the body as the body internally.[41]

This is a wonderfully rich passage, warranting a detailed commentary, but for now I shall offer only a couple of comments. *Introspection* is a mental faculty having the function of monitoring the state of one's body and mind. With this faculty we note when the mind has succumbed to either laxity or excitation, and as soon as we do so, it is imperative to do whatever is necessary to overcome these imbalances. Mindfulness and introspection go hand in hand, as described in the above passage and countless other Buddhist meditation treatises. While the modern Vipassana tradition emphasizes that in the practice of mindfulness we must accept our faults without making any attempt to change them,[42] this advice is a departure from the Buddha's teachings and the writings of the great masters of the past. If you don't balance your attention when it strays into either laxity or excitation, you will only reinforce these mental imbalances, and the quality of your mindfulness will remain flawed indefinitely.

The term *nonobjectification* in this passage refers to no longer clinging to outer objects and events as the true sources of our joys and sorrows. Rather, we see that these feelings arise from our own minds, and this insight heals the mental affliction of avarice and the disappointment that results when our desires are obstructed.

I have known a number of Tibetan Buddhists who have tried to achieve shamatha by focusing on a deliberately generated or visualized mental image, unlike the acquired sign, which arises spontaneously when the mind is sufficiently focused on its meditative object. I tried this approach, too, when I first began practicing shamatha. Many of us—both Asians and Westerners—have found that the effort required to generate and sustain such an image is exhausting. If one practices concentrating on a deliberately visualized image for short periods, there may be no perceptible strain, but if this is done for many hours each day, for day after day, week after week, this can drain your energy and lead to excessive stress and tension. This may be why the Buddha declared that people who are especially prone to excessive conceptualizing should practice shamatha by cultivating mindfulness of breathing. Unlike many other techniques, it soothes the body and mind, rather than constricting them with sustained effort. Even though the mental image of the acquired sign does eventually arise in the practice of mindfulness of breathing, this happens spontaneously, so it does not cause the strain that may result from deliberate visualization.

AN ATTENTIVE WAY OF LIFE

Psychologists have found that the time generally needed to acquire expertise in a variety of high-level skills is five to ten thousand hours of training in a discipline of eight hours each day for fifty weeks in the year. This is roughly the degree of commitment required to progress along the entire path to the achievement of shamatha. Between formal meditation sessions, it is vital to maintain a high degree of mindfulness and introspection throughout the day.

According to Buddhist psychology, when we detect something by way of any of our six senses—vision, hearing, smell, taste, touch, or mental perception—there is a very brief moment before the mind projects concepts and labels onto our immediate experience. Discerning this fraction of a second of pure perception, before concepts, classifications, and emotional responses overlay it, requires a high degree of vividness.[43] This brief instant is important because it is an opportunity for gaining a clearer perception of the nature of phenomena, including a subtle continuum of mental consciousness out of which all forms of sensory perception and conceptualization emerge.

A prominent school of Buddhist psychology states that about six hundred pulselike moments of cognition occur per second, and this accords roughly with modern psychology. These pulses of cognition occur in a continuum very much like frames in a motion picture film. Upon close examination, we discover that our experience is changing each moment. Our fundamental situation is one of change, which is a condition of the body, the mind, the environment, and awareness itself.

Although we have something like six hundred opportunities each second to apprehend some aspect of reality, Buddhist contemplatives and modern psychologists agree that we normally apprehend things at a rate much slower than that. In Buddhism the moments of cognition that don't knowingly engage with anything are called nonascertaining awareness. Appearances arise to the mind, but we don't register them, and afterward we have no recollection of having witnessed them. When we listen closely to music, for example, other sensory impressions, such as extraneous sounds, shapes, colors, and bodily sensations, are still being presented to our awareness, but we note only a very small fraction of them. Attention is highly selective.

Attentional stability is a measure of how many of the ascertained impulses of awareness are focused on our desired object. For example, if we have fifty moments of ascertaining cognition per second and all fifty are focused on the tactile sensations of breathing, this indicates a relatively high degree of stability. A distracted mind, on the other hand, has a high proportion of those fifty ascertaining moments scattered in different fields of perception. Stability is *coherence* with regard to the chosen object. As we relax and our attention stabilizes, if vividness increases, we may experience a higher *density* of moments of ascertaining consciousness each second. The number of ascertaining moments focused on our chosen object may increase, for example, from fifty to a hundred.

During the hypnagogic state of consciousness—a deep state of relaxation as we fall asleep, with our minds withdrawn from the physical senses—there can be a high degree of vividness. I suspect that the exceptional vividness of this transitional phase of consciousness and of some dreams may be due in part to the fact that the mind is relaxed and disengaged from the senses, so there is little competition from other stimuli. But dreams are not usually stable, and we normally have little control in them. That is why the sequence of shamatha training begins with relaxation, then stabilizing attention, and finally maintaining relaxation and stability while gradually increasing vividness.

Many meditators emphasize vividness in their practice because they know that this brings them a kind of "high." But the lasting achievement of vividness has two prerequisites, relaxation and stability. If you want to develop exceptional vividness, first develop relaxation, second develop stability, and then finally increase vividness. Underlying all these aspects of attention must be a foundation of equanimity, without which strong attentional and emotional vacillations will likely persist indefinitely. A general sign of spiritual progress is imperturbability in the face of the vicissitudes of life, and for this, equanimity is the key.

INTERLUDE EQUANIMITY

he cultivation of equanimity serves as an antidote to two of the primary afflictions of the mind: attachment and aversion. Attachment includes clinging to the serenity of shamatha, and aversion can arise by regarding all distractions to your practice, including other people, as disagreeable obstacles to your well-being. The essence of equanimity is impartiality. It is equanimity that allows loving-kindness, compassion, and empathetic joy to expand boundlessly. Normally, these qualities are mixed with attachment, but we grow beyond the mental affliction of attachment as we realize that every sentient being is equally worthy of finding happiness and freedom from suffering.

In Buddhism, a sense of one's self as an immutable, unitary, independent "I" is seen as a root cause of suffering. Clinging to this illusory, autonomous ego leads to the conviction that our own well-being is more important than that of other people. Normally, we live within a set of concentric rings of affection, with ourselves at the center. The first ring out from the center includes our loved ones and dear friends, and the next ring is our circle of friendly acquaintances. Farther out there is a very large ring of people toward whom we feel indifferent. The outermost ring includes people we regard as enemies, people who we believe have obstructed or may obstruct our desires for happiness. This way of prioritizing our feelings for others perpetuates self-centeredness. Equanimity overcomes such self-centeredness and its resultant attachment to and aversion for others.

Events in everyday life can sometimes give us glimpses of equanimity. One such event from my own life occurred when I was teaching at the

University of California at Santa Barbara and was invited to speak at the alternate graduation ceremony. This alternative commencement is a tradition that began in the 1960s when a small group of UCSB students organized a countercultural graduation ceremony in which each student is eulogized by a friend, parent, brother, or sister before receiving his or her diploma. The ceremony goes on and on as you hear how each person is the greatest daughter, the best surfer buddy, the most dedicated activist, the most inspiring friend, or the most cherished lover. Seeing the impression each person has made on someone else, I realized that these graduating students were strangers to me by circumstance only. With just a small shift in circumstances, each one could have been close to me. This is true of everyone in the world. With just a small shift, everyone who seems a stranger to us—each with hopes, fears, and yearnings—could be a dear friend.

When I first moved into a meditation hut high in the mountains above Dharamsala, I went to visit the Tibetan recluse Gen Jhampa Wangdü. In the spring of 1959, shortly after the Tibetan uprising against the Communist invasion of Tibet, Jhampa Wangdü fled his homeland and resumed life as a yogi in India. The day I first dropped by his hermitage made a great impression on me. He was not in strict retreat, so I knew I would not be interfering if I came by during the noon hour. I knocked on his door. A small man who looked a bit like the character Yoda from the movie *Star Wars* opened the door, his face filled with a big, warm smile, as if I were his long-lost son who had finally returned home. He radiated a sense of happiness and kindness. He invited me in and offered me tea. In different circumstances, I might have felt that I was special or that he was especially fond of me. Jhampa Wangdü's compassion and warmth were genuine, but it became obvious to me that his affection was utterly free of personal attachment. I expect anybody would have been received in the same way. But knowing this did not make this reception any less sweet. It was an experience of unconditional love, the key to happiness in any circumstances. This is how reclusive contemplatives maintain their connection to others despite the isolation and hardships of their lives.

Accomplished contemplatives are also remarkably free from impatience. They are free of an "Are we there yet?" attitude. Meditation is their way of life. They may meditate twelve hours or longer each day...until they are enlightened. That is just their daily routine. They aren't waiting for success, gazing longingly at their calendars, hoping for quick results. The Tibetan verb *drupa*, commonly translated as "to practice," also means "to accomplish." When asked, "What are you doing?" a contemplative might answer, "I am practicing/accomplishing shamatha." Practice and achievement are one and the same.

In the circumstances in which most of us find ourselves, with jobs and family responsibilities, it is important to integrate the wisdom of the Buddhist teachings into our lives, so that in the course of our lives, like seasoned contemplatives, we are "practicing/accomplishing." This requires that we adopt a broad sense of what spiritual practice entails. This is not just meditating on a cushion. Resting, walking, or listening to music can be good for the heart, the body, and the mind, and with an altruistic motivation, all of life can become suffused with spiritual practice.

From the perspective of modern psychology, the fact that contemplatives can live in solitude for years without falling into depression, apathy, or mental turmoil is astonishing. Contemplatives are able to do this because they tap into and sustain an inner source of serenity, a source that soothes the body and mind so that all sense of impatience or expectation evaporates. By settling deeply in the calm and luminous stillness of awareness, an inner source of genuine well-being arises that dissipates any sense of loneliness, depression, or mental unease.

The cultivation of equanimity means learning to regard everyone with impartiality. No one is a stranger. When Gen Jhampa Wangdü opened the door to my knock thirty years ago, his heart-warming smile and gracious hospitality radiated equanimity. This is a capacity we can all unveil.

MEDITATION ON EQUANIMITY

After settling your body in its ground state and attending to your breath for a few moments, bring to mind a person you know well, whose background and living circumstances are familiar to you but who is neither a friend nor an enemy. Attend to this person. This person, like yourself, is striving for happiness and freedom from pain, fear, and insecurity. Focus on this person and shift your awareness to view the world from her eyes. From this point of view, look back on yourself. Regardless of the distinct defects or excellent qualities this person might have, her yearning for happiness and wish to be free from pain and grief are identical to your own. Even though she is not close to the center of your personal universe, her well-being is no less significant than that of a dear loved one whom you may regard as crucial to your happiness.

Now bring to mind a person you feel is crucial to your well-being, a person for whom you have both affection and attachment. Attend closely to this loved one, and shift your awareness to the viewpoint of that person so that you perceive him as a human being like yourself, with both defects and excellent qualities. From this viewpoint, realize that although you are loved by some people, a great number of people feel indifferently toward you, and there also may be some people who don't like you. This person for whom you feel affection and attachment feels his own desires, hopes, and fears. Now step back and attend to this person from outside. This person is not a true source of your happiness, security, or joy, which can only arise from your own heart and mind.

Next bring to mind a person who may be intent on bringing you harm or depriving you of happiness, a person with whom you feel conflict. As before, imagine stepping into this person's perspective, being this person from the inside, and experiencing her hopes and fears. Fundamentally, this person, like yourself, wishes to find happiness and freedom from suffering. Now, step back and attend to her from outside with the realization that she is not the source of your distress or anxiety. If you feel uneasy or angry in relationship to this person, the source is in your own heart, not in the other person.

Realize that there is nothing inherent in the stranger, in the loved one, nor in the foe that makes the other person fall into one category or another. Circumstances change, relationships change, and it is the flux of circumstances that gives rise to the thoughts "this is my enemy" or "this is my loved one." Expand the field of awareness to embrace everyone in your immediate environment, their hopes, fears, aspirations, and yearnings. Each person is as important as all others. Shifting circumstances bring us together and also cause us to part. Expand your field of awareness out over the whole community, reaching out in all directions, including everyone. Recognize that each person is fundamentally like yourself, and virtually everyone feels himself to be the center of his world.

Imagine the pure depths of your own awareness, unsullied by the obscurations of self-centered attachment and aversion, as an orb of radiant white light at your heart. With each exhalation, let this light spread out evenly in all directions to all persons with the yearning, "May each one, including myself, find happiness. May everyone, including myself, be free of suffering and the causes of suffering." Imagine a flood of light going out in all directions, soothing those who are distressed and bringing healing, happiness, and a sense of well-being to everyone. With each in-breath, draw in the distress and causes of unhappiness and pain of each sentient being. Imagine this as a dark cloud that dissolves into the light at your heart, and imagine all beings free of suffering and its causes.

Before you bring this session to a close, rest for a moment without bringing anything to mind. Settle your awareness in its own nature, with no object and with no subject. This is the even-mindedness that is a fertile foundation for all spiritual practices.

THE INTERMEDIATE STAGES:
SETTLING THE MIND

STAGE 5: TAMED ATTENTION ● ● ●

Through the skillful, sustained practice of settling the mind in its natural state, eventually you will achieve the fifth attentional stage, called *tamed attention*. At this point, you find that you can take satisfaction in your practice, even though there is still some resistance to it. You have progressed well on this path, and the results of your efforts are apparent to you. Involuntary thoughts continue to arise, but instead of their tumultuous outpouring like a cascading waterfall, they now flow like a river moving smoothly through a gorge.

As you progress from the fourth to the fifth stage of attentional training, you are presented with one of the greatest challenges on the entire path to shamatha. Free of coarse excitation, you must now confront another problem that was lurking in the shadows of your mind all along: coarse laxity. As mentioned earlier, the symptom of this attentional disorder is that your attention succumbs to dullness, which causes it to largely disengage from its meditative object. The Tibetan word for laxity has the connotation of *sinking*. It's as if the attention, instead of rising to the object, sinks down from it into the recesses of the mind. The attention fades, as it were, but instead of fading out, it's more like fading in, stepping onto a slippery slope that leads down to sluggishness, lethargy, and finally sleep. This is a peaceful state of mind, so the ignorant may mistake it for the attainment of shamatha, which literally means quiescence, tranquillity, and serenity. True shamatha is imbued not only with a degree of stability far beyond that achieved at this stage of attentional practice but also with an extraordinary vividness that one has hardly begun to develop at this point in the training.

In the fifth stage, you rise to the challenge of overcoming coarse laxity without destabilizing your attention. In addition to the persistent problem of medium excitation—which arises when involuntary thoughts occupy the center of attention while the meditative object is displaced to the periphery—you now have the task of recognizing and counteracting a medium degree of laxity. When this degree of laxity sets in, the object of meditation appears, but without much vividness. This is subtly different from coarse laxity, and you will discover that distinction only through practice.

The primary challenge here is to overcome laxity without undermining stability. The way to counteract laxity is to arouse the attention, to take a greater interest in the object of meditation. Tibetan contemplatives liken this to stringing a lute. If the strings are too taut, they may easily break under the strain, but if they are too slack, the instrument is unplayable. Likewise, the task at this point is to determine the proper "pitch" of attention. If you arouse the mind too much in your efforts to remedy laxity, it will easily fall into excitation, but if you relax too much, you will likely succumb to laxity. It's a delicate balancing act, and the only way you can meet this challenge is through your own experience, determining for yourself the suitable degree of effort to tune your attention. Buddhist contemplatives have grappled with this dilemma for millennia, and they report that it takes great skill to solve it.

Having achieved the third and fourth stages with the power of mindfulness, the fifth stage is achieved by the power of introspection. The *power of introspection* is the faculty of monitoring the quality of your attention, and this skill must now be honed so that you can detect more and more subtle degrees of laxity and excitation. The Buddha referred to this function of introspection as follows:[44]

> Herein a monk should constantly review his own mind thus: "Does any excitation concerning these five cords of sensual pleasure ever arise in me on any occasion?" If, on reviewing his mind, the monk understands: "Excitation concerning these five cords of sensual pleasure does arise in me on certain occasions," then he understands: "Desire and lust for the five cords of sensual pleasure

are not abandoned in me." In this way he has introspection of that. But if, on reviewing his mind, the monk understands: "No excitation concerning these five cords of sensual pleasure arises in me on any occasion," then he understands: "Desire and lust for the five cords of sensual pleasure are abandoned in me." In this way he has introspection of that.

Buddhaghosa drew this distinction between mindfulness and introspection: "Mindfulness has the characteristic of remembering. Its function is not to forget. It is manifested as guarding. Introspection has the characteristic of non-confusion. Its function is to investigate. It is manifested as scrutiny."[45] And his contemporary Asanga offers a view that is strikingly similar: "Mindfulness and introspection are taught, for the first prevents the attention from straying from the meditative object, while the second recognizes that the attention is straying."[46] Shantideva's definition of introspection appears to reflect both these views: "In brief, this alone is the definition of introspection: the repeated examination of the state of one's body and mind."[47] Throughout Buddhist literature, the training in shamatha is often likened to training a wild elephant, and the two primary instruments for this are the tether of mindfulness and the goad of introspection.

Buddhist psychology classifies introspection as a form of intelligence (prajna), and its development has long been an important element of Buddhist meditation. A similar mental faculty, usually called metacognition, is now coming under the scrutiny of modern psychologists. Cognitive researchers have defined metacognition as knowledge of one's own cognitive and affective processes and states, as well as the ability to consciously and deliberately monitor and regulate those processes and states.[48] This appears to be an especially rich area for collaborative research between Buddhist contemplatives and cognitive scientists.

This phase of the path to shamatha also brings you to a major fork in the road. You may continue in the practice of mindfulness of breathing, which is so strongly recommended for overcoming excitation. Many Buddhist contemplatives have encouraged meditators who are determined to achieve shamatha to continue practicing with just one object. But Padmasambhava, the Indian master instrumental in first bringing Buddhism to Tibet, encouraged the use of multiple methods to counter the tenacious impediments to the achievement of shamatha.[49] There are merits to both views. It is very easy to grow bored or dissatisfied with your meditative object in this practice and to then fish around for other more interesting, and hopefully more effective, techniques. You may easily be enticed by highly esoteric, secret practices, thinking that they will be more effective than the one you are engaging in now. Such roving from one meditation object and technique to another, always on the prowl for a greater "bang for your buck," can undermine any sustained practice of shamatha. Repeatedly experimenting with different techniques can prevent you from achieving expertise in any of them.

I shall set forth here the option of advancing to another method after you have achieved the fourth stage by mindfulness of breathing. This is the practice of *settling the mind in its natural state*, a technique that directly prepares you for Mahamudra and Dzogchen practice, two traditions of contemplative practice that are focused on the realization of the nature of consciousness. A comparable practice within the Theravada tradition is called "unfastened mindfulness."[50]

Like mindfulness of breathing, this method is especially suited for people whose minds are prone to excitation and conceptual turbulence, and it has the further advantage of providing deep insight into the nature of the mind. Düdjom Lingpa, a Tibetan Dzogchen master of the late nineteenth and early twentieth century, commented that this practice may be the most suitable for high-strung people with unstable minds who may run into great difficulties by adopting various visualization techniques for developing shamatha.[51] The First Panchen Lama, a teacher of the Fifth Dalai Lama, referred to this practice as "a wonderfully skillful method for novices to still the mind."[52]

You *can* begin your shamatha practice with this method and continue with it all the way to the achievement of shamatha. You don't need to practice mindfulness of breathing first. However, many people find this method difficult, as they are swept away time and again by their thoughts. For them, mindfulness of breathing may be the most effective way to progress along the first four stages on this path.

While many people practice meditation to achieve "altered states of consciousness," from a Buddhist perspective, our habitual mindsets, in which we are drawn under the influence of such imbalances as craving, anxiety, stress, and frustration, are *already* altered states of consciousness. The practice of settling the mind in its natural state is designed to release us from these habitual perturbations of consciousness, letting the mind gradually settle in its ground state. The "natural state" of the mind, according to Buddhist contemplatives, is characterized by the three qualities of bliss, luminosity, and nonconceptuality. I believe this is one of the most remarkable discoveries ever made concerning the nature of consciousness, and that it calls for collaborative research between cognitive scientists and contemplatives.

For a description of this practice, I shall cite the essential instructions given by the nineteenth-century Dzogchen master Lerab Lingpa.[53] His instructions are presented here, followed by my own detailed commentary.

THE PRACTICE: SETTLING THE MIND IN ITS NATURAL STATE

Simply hearing your spiritual mentor's practical instructions and knowing how to explain them to others does not liberate your own mindstream, so you must meditate. Even if you spend your whole life practicing a mere semblance of meditation—meditating in a stupor, cluttering the mind with fantasies, and taking many breaks during your sessions due to being unable to control mental scattering—no good experiences or realizations will arise. So it is important during each session to meditate according to your mentor's oral instructions.

In solitude sit upright on a comfortable cushion. Gently hold the "vase" breath until the vital energies converge naturally. Let your gaze be vacant. With your body and mind inwardly relaxed, and without allowing the continuum of your consciousness to fade from a state of limpidity and vivid clarity, sustain it naturally and radiantly. Do not clutter your mind with many critical judgments; do not take a shortsighted view of meditation, and avoid great hopes and fears that your meditation will turn out one way and not another. At the beginning have many daily sessions, each of them of brief duration, and focus well in each one. Whenever you meditate, bear in mind the phrase "without distraction and without grasping," and put this into practice.

As you gradually familiarize yourself with the meditation, increase the duration of your sessions. If dullness sets in, arouse your awareness. If there is excessive scattering and excitation, loosen up. Determine in terms of your own experience the optimal degree of mental arousal, as well as the healthiest diet and behavior.

Excessive, imprisoning constriction of the mind, loss of clarity due to lassitude, and excessive relaxation resulting in involuntary vocalization and eye-movement are to be avoided. It does only harm to talk a lot about such things as extrasensory perception and miscellaneous dreams or to claim, "I saw a deity. I saw a ghost. I know this. I've realized that," and so on. The presence or absence of any kind of pleasure or displeasure, such as a sensation of motion, is not uniform, for there are great differences in the dispositions and faculties from one individual to another.

Due to maintaining the mind in its natural state, there may arise sensations such as physical and mental well-being, a sense of lucid consciousness, the appearance of empty forms, and a non-conceptual sense that nothing can harm the mind, regardless of whether or not thoughts have ceased. Whatever kinds of mental imagery occur—be they gentle or violent, subtle or coarse, of long or short duration, strong or weak, good or bad—observe their nature, and avoid any obsessive evaluation of them as being one thing and not another. Let the heart of your practice be consciousness in its natural state, limpid and vivid. Acting as your own mentor, if you can bring the essential points to perfection, as if you were threading a needle, the afflictions of your own mindstream will subside, you will gain the autonomy of not succumbing to them, and your mind will constantly be calm and dispassionate.

This is a sound basis for the arising of all states of meditative concentration on the stages of generation and completion.

This is like tilling the soil of a field. So from the outset avoid making a lot of great, exalted, and pointless proclamations. Rather, it is crucial to do all you can to refine your mind and establish a foundation for contemplative practice.[54]

REFLECTIONS ON THE PRACTICE

The object of mindfulness in the practice of settling the mind in its natural state is no longer the subtle sensations of the breath at the nostrils, but the *space of the mind* and whatever events arise within that space. The object of introspection, as in the earlier practice of mindfulness of breathing, is the quality of the attention with which you are observing the mind.

At the beginning have many daily sessions, each of them of brief duration, and focus well in each one. Whenever you meditate, bear in mind the phrase "without distraction and without grasping," and put this into practice.

As you venture into this practice, I would encourage you to memorize these quintessential instructions: settle your mind without distraction and without grasping. Practicing "without distraction" means not allowing your mind to be carried away by thoughts and sense impressions. Be present here and now, and when thoughts arise pertaining to the past or future or ruminations about the present, don't be abducted by them. As you hike on this trail of shamatha, don't be a hitchhiker, catching a ride with any of the thoughts or images that whiz through your mind. Rather, be like a kestrel, hovering motionlessly as it faces the wind, slightly moving its wings and tail feathers to adjust to changes in the currents of the air.

Even when your attention is settled in the present, you may still grasp onto the appearances to the mind. Whenever you prefer one mental object over another, whenever you try to control the contents of your mind, and whenever you identify with anything at all, grasping has set it. Here is the challenge at hand: be attentive to everything that comes up in the mind, but don't grasp onto anything. In this practice, let your mind be like the sky. Whatever moves through it, the sky never reacts. It doesn't stop anything from moving through it, it doesn't hold onto anything that's present, nor does it control anything. The sky doesn't prefer rainbows to clouds, butterflies to jet planes. Whatever comes up in the field of awareness, without distraction or grasping, just let it be.

When you are settling the mind in its natural state, occasionally falling into distraction or grasping, you experience a semblance of what it is like to fall from the state of pristine awareness (Tibetan: *rigpa*) into the mind of dualistic grasping. This is not something that occurred long ago in a Buddhist Garden of Eden. It happens each moment that the dualistic mind is activated and we lose sight of our own true nature. Pristine awareness is always present. But it is obscured when we become carried away by the objects that captivate our attention, and to which we respond with craving and aversion.

> As you gradually familiarize yourself with the meditation, increase the duration of your sessions. If dullness sets in, arouse your awareness. If there is excessive scattering and excitation, loosen up.

This is the essential guidance on how to remedy laxity and excitation as soon as you've noted these imbalances with your faculty of introspection. If you feel a natural urge to constrict the mind when it becomes agitated, overcome this urge and loosen up. Let the stability of your attention emerge naturally from the mind at ease, rather than a mind that is strenuously constricted. But see that your mind is not so slack that dullness sets in. Here is the challenge, mentioned earlier, that is especially characteristic of the transition from the fourth to the fifth attentional stage. With fine-honed introspection, you quickly detect attentional imbalances, and you then take the necessary measures to restore balance.

> Simply hearing your spiritual mentor's practical instructions and knowing how to explain them to others does not liberate your

own mindstream, so you must meditate. Even if you spend your whole life practicing a mere semblance of meditation—meditating in a stupor, cluttering the mind with fantasies, and taking many breaks during your sessions due to being unable to control mental scattering—no good experiences or realizations will arise. So it is important during each session to meditate according to your mentor's oral instructions.

While much can be learned from books about meditation—and this can be enough to get you started—for dedicated, sustained practice there is no substitute for a knowledgeable, experienced teacher. This is true for professional training in the cognitive sciences—there are no expert psychologists or neuroscientists who are entirely self-taught—and in a myriad of other fields. It is possible to waste an enormous amount of time in faulty meditative practice, and there is also the possibility of damaging your mind, so it is important to find qualified instructors and to listen closely to their counsel. As the Dalai Lama responded when asked whether it is necessary to have a teacher in order to achieve enlightenment, "No, but it can save you a lot of time!"

In solitude sit upright on a comfortable cushion.

Sitting upright with legs crossed is generally the most suitable posture for meditation, and many meditation manuals give detailed instructions on the specific points of such a posture.[55] But Lerab Lingpa also advised that you be comfortable when meditating. So if sitting cross-legged for extended periods is painful for you, try sitting in a chair or lying in the supine position. Düdjom Lingpa gave this advice:[56]

Motionlessly relax your body in whatever way is comfortable, like an unthinking corpse in a charnel ground. Let your voice be silent like a lute with its strings cut. Rest your mind in an unmodified state, like the primordial presence of space.... Remain for a long time in [this way] of resting. This pacifies all illnesses due to disturbances of the elements and unfavorable circumstances, and your body, speech, and mind naturally calm down.

Lerab Lingpa continues:

> Gently hold the vase breath until the vital energies converge naturally.

"Vase breathing" is an energizing and stabilizing breath practice. To practice "gentle vase breathing," as you inhale, let the sensations of the breath flow down to the bottom of your abdomen, like pouring water into a vase. Then, as you exhale, instead of letting the abdomen retract completely, keep it slightly rounded, with your belly soft. In this way, you maintain a bit of a potbelly, which expands during the in-breath and contracts somewhat during the out-breath, but still retains a fullness. The goal of the vase breath is to converge the vital energies, or *pranas*, in the central channel in your abdomen and allow them to settle in this region. This is something you can detect from your own direct experience of your body and the movement of energies within it. When you settle your mind in its natural state, opening up the abdomen with such breathing, the *pranas* start to converge naturally into the central channel that runs vertically through the torso to the crown of the head. Most explanations of shamatha practice make no reference to vase breathing, so it is not indispensable. But many people do find it helpful for stabilizing the mind and tuning the subtle energies in the body.

> Let your gaze be vacant.

In this practice, it is important that your eyes are open, vacantly resting your gaze in the space in front of you. If you have not meditated with your eyes open, you may find this uncomfortable, but I encourage you to get used to it. Blink as often as you like and don't strain your eyes in any way. Let them be as relaxed as if you were daydreaming with your eyes open. By leaving the eyes open, while focusing your attention on the domain of mental events, the artificial barrier between "inner" and "outer" begins to dissolve. Especially in our materialist society, we have gotten used to the idea that our thoughts and all other mental events are inside our heads. But this has never been demonstrated scientifically. All that is known in this regard is that mental events are correlated with neural events, but that doesn't necessarily mean that they are located in the same place.

Even without this materialist assumption that the mind is nothing more than a function of the brain, we naturally have a sense that we are looking out on the world from behind our eyes. But this sense of an independent subject, or ego, inside the head is an illusion. There is no scientific support for such a belief, and when it is inspected through rigorous contemplative inquiry, this autonomous thinker and observer inside the head is nowhere to be found. In this practice, by leaving your eyes open but directing your attention to the mind, this conceptually superimposed demarcation between inner and outer begins to erode. You begin to recognize that your thoughts are not occurring in here, in your head, nor are they occurring out there in space. This practice challenges the existence of an absolutely objective space of the physical senses that is absolutely separate from a subjective space of the mind. You are now on a path to realizing the meaning of nonduality.

> With your body and mind inwardly relaxed, and without allow-
> ing the continuum of your consciousness to fade from a state of
> limpidity and vivid clarity, sustain your awareness naturally and
> radiantly.

On the path of shamatha, while it is crucial to enhance both the stability and vividness of attention, this must not be done at the expense of relaxation. On the foundation of bodily and mental ease, let the stability of your attention deepen, and from that increasing stillness, witness the natural vividness of awareness. The *limpidity* of consciousness refers to its qualities of transparency and luminosity. The space of the mind is limpid, like a pool of transparent, brightly lit water. Clarity, limpidity, and radiance are qualities of awareness itself, not qualities added to it by meditation. So this practice is one of discovering, not developing, the innate stillness and vividness of awareness.

> Do not clutter your mind with many critical judgments; do not
> take a shortsighted view of meditation, and avoid great hopes
> and fears that your meditation will turn out one way and not
> another.

One of the most helpful pieces of advice my spiritual mentor, Gyatrul Rinpoche, gave me had to do with hope and desire. He told me that when I was meditating, I was doing so with too much yearning. "But," I countered, "I've been told many times about the importance of developing a strong motivation for practice, and this entails desiring to succeed. So how is it possible to cultivate a powerful yearning to practice, then do with little or no desire?"

He responded, "Between sessions, it is fine to meditate on the value of such practice and to arouse your motivation to engage in it with great diligence. But during your meditation sessions themselves, let go of all such desires. Release your hopes and your fears, and simply devote yourself to the practice, moment by moment." Especially in the modern West, where so many people are in a hurry, intent on finding quick fixes and short-term gains, it is easy to take a shortsighted view of meditation. It is a big mistake to judge the value of meditation solely on the basis of how good you feel while meditating. This isn't a miracle drug designed to provide temporary relief within minutes. It's a path to greater and greater sanity, and for that we have to be patient and persevering.

> Determine in terms of your own experience the optimal degree
> of mental arousal, as well as the healthiest diet and behavior.

As the practice becomes subtler, you have to discover for yourself the optimal degree of mental arousal, or tension. Video-game players commonly experience a high state of mental arousal, while in deep sleep we all experience the opposite state of low arousal. Recall the analogy of stringing a lute: like finding the optimal degree of tension on the strings, determine the optimal degree of arousal of your attention.

In addition, since your meditating mind is embodied, it is crucial to determine from your own experience the healthiest diet and daily behavior. Eat small, nutritious meals, suitable for your own physical constitution, and exercise in a way that keeps your body fit. Walking is good exercise between sessions, but very strong aerobic exercise may agitate your nervous system and mind in ways that detract from the practice. Experiment for yourself to see what kind of diet and exercise best support your practice.

> Excessive, imprisoning constriction of the mind, loss of clarity due to lassitude, and excessive relaxation resulting in involuntary vocalization and eye-movement are to be avoided.

Settling the mind in its natural state, like all shamatha practices, is a balancing act. If you constrict the mind too much, you will become exhausted and stressed out. If you let your mind go too slack, the clarity of attention will fade, resulting in involuntary vocal and bodily activity.

> It does only harm to talk a lot about such things as extrasensory perception and miscellaneous dreams or to claim, "I saw a deity. I saw a ghost. I know this. I've realized that," and so on. The presence or absence of any kind of pleasure or displeasure, such as a sensation of motion, is not uniform, for there are great differences in the dispositions and faculties from one individual to another.

A wide range of physical and mental experiences may arise in the course of this practice. Some of them may be inspiring, for example, when you feel you've broken through to a profound mystical insight, while others may be troubling or simply weird. While many Westerners love to report their meditative experiences to others, this runs against the grain of traditional Buddhist practice. Tibetans have an old saying: If you fill a gourd with just a little water and shake it, it makes a lot of noise. But if you fill it to the brim and shake it, it makes no sound. Generations of seasoned contemplatives have found that making any claims about one's spiritual achievements— even if they are true—creates obstacles to one's practice. These are private matters, and if you discuss them with anyone, it should be in private with your own spiritual mentor.

> Due to maintaining the mind in its natural state, there may arise
> sensations such as physical and mental well-being, a sense of
> lucid consciousness, the appearance of empty forms, and a non-
> conceptual sense that nothing can harm the mind, regardless of
> whether or not thoughts have ceased.

When the body and mind are in a state of imbalance, we feel uncomfortable. This is a good thing, otherwise we wouldn't do anything to remedy
the problem. All too often, though, instead of seeking a cure, we look for
quick fixes to suppress the symptoms. The path of shamatha leads to
increasing mental balance, and we may experience that as physical and
mental well-being. As the dust of the mind settles, you may discover an
unprecedented degree of lucidity of awareness. Moreover, as the deeply
ingrained habit of conceptual grasping subsides, you may begin to experience physical objects in a different way. Normally, the mind involuntarily
superimposes a sense of solidity on our perceptions of visual objects, even
though the eyes are not designed to detect this tactile characteristic. As
the conceptual mind calms down, you will see more clearly what the
Buddha meant when he said, "In the seen there is only the seen." Visual
objects are seen simply as visual objects, without the overlay of past experiences of substantiality. Sensory objects take on a quality of transparency,
as mere appearances to the mind, rather than solid objects "out there." Even
your own body appears "empty" of substance. All that appears to the mind
is an interrelated matrix of sensory phenomena, but these qualities no
longer appear to belong to something absolutely objective, for that sense
of reified duality is diminishing.

Another remarkable experience that may arise from this practice is a
nonconceptual sense that nothing can harm the mind regardless of
whether or not thoughts have ceased. This implies that even when concepts are present, your awareness may remain nonconceptual. How is this
possible? Normally, when thoughts appear, you may normally grasp onto
them, often only semiconsciously, and your attention is directed to the
referents of the thoughts. For example, if a mental image of your mother
comes up, you start thinking about your mother. Or if memories arise of

someone ridiculing you, out of habit your mind goes back to that occasion, rekindling the emotions you felt at the time and thereby reinforcing them. But in this practice, whatever thoughts or mental images arise, you simply observe them, without distraction and without grasping. You nonconceptually note them as mental events in the present, without attending to their referents and without being either attracted to them or repulsed by them. You just let them be. In this way you can maintain a nonconceptual awareness of concepts.

As the old saying goes, "Sticks and stones can break your bones," but appearances to the mind cannot harm you if you don't grasp onto them, identify with them, and thereby empower them. As you settle the mind in its natural state—which is profoundly different from its habitual, dualistic state of distraction and grasping—you will find that it heals itself and unveils its own inner resources of well-being. Gyatrul Rinpoche told me, "When your mind is settled in its natural state, even if a thousand demons were to rise up to attack you, they could not harm you. And even if a thousand buddhas appeared to you in a vision, you would not need their blessing." When your mind is free of grasping, it provides no target; it can be harmed no more than the sky can be harmed by a missile attack. And when your mind is settled in its natural state, you discover for yourself the innate qualities of bliss, luminosity, and stillness that have always been there.

> Whatever kinds of mental imagery occur—be they gentle or violent, subtle or coarse, of long or short duration, strong or weak, good or bad—observe their nature, and avoid any obsessive evaluation of them as being one thing and not another.

In the practice of mindfulness of breathing, you are faced with the challenge of carefully observing, *without controlling*, sensations within the body associated with the breathing. Now you face a similar challenge of carefully observing events within the mind without regulating or evaluating them in any way. A Tibetan aphorism states, "Let your mind be a gracious host in the midst of unruly guests." In the shamatha practice of mindfulness of breathing, you let go of thoughts as soon as you detect them and return your attention to the breath. But now, instead of letting thoughts *go*, you let them *be*. Don't prefer one kind of thought to another. Avoid all kinds of attraction to and repulsion from any mental imagery. Don't even prefer the absence of thoughts to the presence of thoughts. They are not the problem. Being distracted by and grasping onto thoughts is the problem. Recognize this crucial difference from the preceding practice.

With mindfulness of breathing, you measured the stability of your attention with respect to a continuous object—sensations of the breath. But when settling the mind in its natural state, thoughts are anything but continuous. They come and go sporadically, so the stability of attention is not in relation to a specific object. It's a quality of your subjective awareness. Even when thoughts are on the move, because you are not distracted by them and don't grasp onto them, your awareness remains still. This is called the *fusion of stillness and movement.*

During the course of this training, you will experience periods when your mind seems to be empty. Thoughts and mental images seem to have disappeared. This is a time to arouse the vividness of your attention to see if you can detect subtle mental events that have been lurking just beneath the threshold of your awareness. This is one reason for switching to this technique after you have achieved the fourth attentional stage: you are continually challenged to arouse the clarity of attention, but without losing its stability. Watch closely, but continue to breathe normally. Don't let the intensity of your awareness impede the natural flow of your respiration. If, even under the closest scrutiny, you don't detect any appearances in the space of your mental awareness, simply be aware of that empty space. The object of meditation in this practice is both the space of the mind and anything that arises within it. So you can always continue to practice, with or without distinct appearances arising in the mind.

> Let the heart of your practice be consciousness in its natural state,
> limpid and vivid. Acting as your own mentor, if you can bring the
> essential points to perfection, as if you were threading a needle,
> the afflictions of your own mindstream will subside, you will gain
> the autonomy of not succumbing to them, and your mind will

constantly be calm and dispassionate. This is a sound basis for the arising of all states of meditative concentration on the stages of generation and completion.

While it is very helpful to practice under the guidance of a qualified teacher, when you are on your cushion, you need to be your own mentor, implementing the teachings given you by your mentor. This is a delicate practice, like threading a needle, not a Herculean effort like weight lifting. Recognize that in the practice of shamatha, "doing your best" doesn't mean "trying your hardest." If you're trying your hardest, you're trying too hard and you'll burn out if you persist in that way. By cultivating shamatha with intelligence, perceptiveness, patience, and enthusiasm, none of your mental afflictions will be healed irreversibly. They will still arise from time to time, but the more you advance, the more those afflictions will subside and the greater autonomy you will have from them. The result is increasing emotional balance and equanimity. Your psychological immune system is strengthened, so when events occur that were previously upsetting, you can now deal with them with greater composure. Your mind remains calm and it is not dominated by the passions of craving and hostility. This is a clear indication of heightened sanity. The "stages of generation and completion" mentioned above are the two phases of Buddhist tantric practice, and Lerab Lingpa points out here that success in this shamatha technique provides a sound basis for all such advanced meditative practices.

> This is like tilling the soil of a field. So from the outset avoid making a lot of great, exalted, and pointless proclamations. Rather, it is crucial to do all you can to refine your mind and establish a foundation for contemplative practice.

With these words, Lerab Lingpa concludes his quintessential instructions on settling the mind in its natural state. The achievement of shamatha by way of such practice is not the final fruition of Buddhist practice, any more than cultivating a field is the same as reaping its harvest. But such refinement of the mind is an essential foundation for later practices that are designed to unveil the deepest potentials of consciousness.

.

INTERLUDE TONGLEN—"GIVING AND TAKING"

The first four interludes have focused on the meditative cultivation of loving-kindness, compassion, empathetic joy, and equanimity, which together provide a wonderful array of practices for opening the heart and achieving emotional equilibrium. These are much-needed auxiliary practices for the development of shamatha, and they are deeply meaningful in their own right. We move now to the Mahayana practice of *tonglen*, which literally means "giving and taking." This one method integrates loving-kindness and compassion on a foundation of equanimity, and in so doing, it uplifts the mind that falls into depression and calms the mind that gets caught up in emotional turbulence. Just as mindfulness of a single cycle of respiration—arousing the attention during the in-breath and relaxing during the out-breath—wards off attentional laxity and excitation, so does *tonglen* counteract emotional imbalances of depression and excitement. And when it is conjoined with breathing, it can be especially effective.

TONGLEN MEDITATION

After settling your body and mind in their natural states, symbolically imagine your own pristine awareness—transcending all distortions and afflictions of the mind—as an orb of radiant white light, about a half inch in diameter, in the center of your chest. Visualize this orb as a fathomless source of loving-kindness and compassion, as a light of unlimited goodness and joy. This is the healing power of awareness. Now bring to mind the difficulties in your life, the kinds of suffering you bear, together with the inner causes of such distress. Imagine these as a dark cloud that obscures your deepest nature and obstructs your pursuit of genuine happiness. With the compassionate yearning, "May I be free of suffering and its causes," with each in-breath, imagine drawing this darkness into the light at your heart, where it is extinguished without trace. With each breath, imagine this darkness being dispelled, and experience the relief of this burden being lightened.

Now bring to mind your vision of your own flourishing as a human being. Imagine the blessings you would love to receive from the world, and imagine the ways in which you would love to become transformed so that you may experience the fulfillment you seek. Then with the aspiration, "May I find happiness and its causes," with each out-breath, visualize light flowing from the inexhaustible source at your heart, permeating every cell of your body and every facet of your mind. Imagine this light permeating your whole being, fulfilling your heart's longing with each exhalation.

Next, invite into the field of your awareness someone you dearly love. Apply the previous practice to this person, compassionately drawing in the darkness of his suffering and its causes with each in-breath, and lovingly sending forth the light of happiness and its causes with each out-breath. As you do so, imagine this person being freed from suffering and discovering the genuine happiness that he seeks.

After dissolving the appearance of your loved one back into the space of your awareness, invoke the memory of someone toward whom you feel relatively indifferent, and practice in the same way with the recognition that this person's suffering and well-being are just as real and important as those of yourself and your loved ones.

In the next phase of this practice, follow the same steps either with a person who has harmed you or those you love, or with someone whom you dislike, perhaps because of her deplorable behavior. With each in-breath, make a special point of drawing in the darkness of the causes of this person's suffering—such as greed, hostility, and delusion—which may also indirectly harm many other people as well. With each inhalation, imagine this person becoming freed from these harmful tendencies, and with each exhalation, imagine her finding genuine happiness, while cultivating its true causes.

Before you bring this meditation to a close, you may open your awareness in all directions, enfolding all sentient beings within the field of your loving-kindness and compassion. With each breath, compassionately draw in the world's darkness of suffering and its causes, and lovingly suffuse the world with the light of happiness and its causes. In the final moments of this meditation, release all desires and images, and simply rest your awareness in the present moment, with no object. Just be present.

STAGE 6: PACIFIED ATTENTION ● ● ●

As you continue in the full-time practice of shamatha, after some thousands of hours of rigorous training, you will reach the sixth attentional stage, known as *pacified attention*. This is achieved by the power of introspection, and by now you no longer experience resistance to the training. You must still be on guard against the occurrence of medium laxity, in which you are aware of the object of mindfulness, but it is not very vivid. In addition, you are now prone to and need to be able to detect subtle excitation, in which the meditative object remains at the center of attention, but involuntary thoughts emerge at the periphery. Returning to our earlier metaphor of listening to the radio, this is like being tuned to the desired station but faintly hearing another station, or simply static, at the same time. The quality of attention you are seeking here is like a clear channel, unsullied with extraneous noise.

In stage six, involuntary thoughts pass through your consciousness like a river slowly flowing through a valley. As the mind becomes more at ease, thoughts flicker like butterflies through the space of awareness, and you are able to passively witness the entire sequence of thoughts arising, playing themselves out, then vanishing. They seem to be less "weighty" in that they are less able to pull your attention after them. Like Einstein's theory that physical space is warped by bodies of matter within it, it sometimes feels as if the space of awareness is warped by the contents of the mind. At times, when we become fixated on something, our minds seem to become very small. Trivial issues loom up in our awareness as if they were very large and important. In reality, they haven't become large. Our minds have become small. The experienced magnitude of the contents of the mind is relative to the spaciousness of the mind. So to keep the activities of the mind in perspective, let the space of awareness remain as expansive as possible. In the meantime, the less you grasp onto mental events, the less the space of the mind contracts around them and is warped by them.

Throughout the development of shamatha, even at this relatively advanced stage, a myriad of emotions and other mental and physical conditions may arise, many of them very unexpectedly. This practice of settling the mind in its natural state is especially known for unveiling the suppressed and repressed contents of the mind, and these vary widely from one individual to the next. There is no way to predict beforehand what kinds of experiences you may have.

One of the more common challenges in this practice is the emergence of fear. As you release your grip on the contents of the mind, you are undermining your normal sense of personal identity, which is constantly reinforced by thinking, by recalling and identifying with your personal history, hopes, and plans. Now you are disengaging from these familiar supports for substantiating your ego. As lapses between thoughts occur more and more frequently and for longer periods, your awareness hovers in a kind of empty space, a vacuum devoid of personhood. You may come into the grip of fear as your normal sense of who you are loses its footing. The teacher Gen Lamrimpa warned his students that such dread may well arise during their training. It is crucial, he counseled, not to identify with it, nor to give it any credence. Some kinds of fear are based in reality. They protect us from danger, filling the body with energy so that we can flee or protect ourselves in whatever way necessary. But this kind of dread, with no clear object, has no such basis in reality. There is no danger in the empty, luminous space of awareness. You have nothing to lose but your false sense of an independent, controlling ego. The only thing being threatened is an illusion. If you don't identify with it, there's nothing to fear. If you do identify with this fear, it may bring your entire practice to a grinding halt and throw you into deep emotional imbalances. So it is of the utmost importance to observe such fear without distraction and without grasping. Keep to the essentials of the practice.

Another emotional imbalance that may crop up at any time throughout this training is depression, which may be related to a deep-rooted sense of guilt and low self-esteem. When any of these emotions or attitudes arise during meditation sessions, treat them like any other mental event: watch their emergence, see how they linger, then observe them disappear back into the space of the mind. Examine them with discerning intelligence, but without any emotional charge. Rather than identifying with them, or owning them, let them emerge from the space of awareness and dissolve back, without any intervention on your part—even without any preference for them to go away. Let the space of your mind be emotionally neutral, like physical space, which could not care less whether bullets or hummingbirds streak through it.

THE PRACTICE: SETTLING THE MIND IN ITS NATURAL STATE— PLUMBING THE DEPTHS

When you first begin the practice of settling the mind in its natural state, you may have difficulty identifying the intangible domain of the mind. Or even if you do settle your awareness there, after some time your attention may become vague, disoriented, or spaced out. If you have difficulty identifying the domain of the mind or sustaining attention there, consciously bring up a thought such as, "What is the mind?" and attend to it. Don't think about this question or try to answer it. Just observe the thought itself, watching it emerge in the field of consciousness and then dissolve back into that space. Once it's gone, keep your focus right where the thought was and see what comes up next. If you slip back into a kind of lax, mindless vacuity, deliberately generate the thought again, and observe it with bare attention. When you become familiar with this practice, you will no longer need to generate such a thought to crystallize your awareness and locate your attention. That will happen by itself as thoughts arise and pass of their own accord.

The practice of attending to the space of the mind and whatever events arise there is like taking a naturalist's field trip into the wilderness of your mind. When you first embark on this inward journey, you may perceive very little. But as you grow more accustomed to the practice, you will begin to identify an increasing quantity and range of mental phenomena. Some of them are discrete, like thoughts and images, while others are nebulous, like emotions and moods. This practice provides you with experiential access to a domain that cannot be observed with any of the instruments of modern science or technology. The most they can do is detect the neural and behavioral correlates of the phenomena you are observing directly. You have become a naturalist of the mind, and a whole new world is opening up to you that for most people remains largely unconscious.

In this practice, the locus of awareness gradually descends from the superficial level of the coarse mental activity that is immediately accessible through introspection down into the inner recesses of the mind that are normally below the threshold of consciousness. You discover in this training that the border between conscious and unconscious mental events shifts in relation to the degrees of relaxation, stability, and vividness of attention. Especially when you engage in this practice for many hours each day, for days, weeks, or months at a time, you dredge the depths of your own psyche. In doing so, you remember long-forgotten experiences, both pleasant and unpleasant, and a wide range of desires and emotions.

What happens here is a kind of luminously clear, discerning, free association of thoughts, mental images, memories, desires, fantasies, and emotions. You are plumbing the depths of your own mind, undistracted by external diversions. Once-hidden phenomena are unmasked through the lack of suppression of whatever comes up. This is potentially an extraordinarily deep kind of therapy, and the more intensively you practice it, the more important it is to proceed under the guidance of an experienced, compassionate teacher. During your meditation sessions, internalize the wisdom of this contemplative tradition and make sure that you implement the core instructions of this practice: whatever arises in the mind, do not be carried away by it, and do not grasp onto or identify with it. Just let it be. Watch thoughts, feelings, or other mental events arise, with discerning intelligence be aware of their nature, and let them slip back into the space of awareness without any judgment or intervention on your part. This is the key to letting the knots of the psyche unravel themselves as the extraordinary healing capacity of the mind reveals itself. This is the path to deep sanity.

REFLECTIONS ON THE PRACTICE

At the beginning of a one-year training held in Washington State in 1988, Gen Lamrimpa warned participants that they might experience visions of demons or other terrifying apparitions. Many Tibetan contemplatives have reported such experiences while engaging in prolonged, intensive practice, and the existence of such nonhuman beings is very much part of the traditional Buddhist worldview. As it turned out, no one during the retreat, as far as I know, reported seeing any such apparitions, possibly because belief in their existence is not so common in modern Western society. But some of the participants were plagued at times with the "demons" of lust, spiritual arrogance, fear, boredom, self-doubt, guilt, and low self-esteem. While science has apparently swept the objective, physical world clean of all gods, spirits, and demons, the subjective world of the mind continues to be densely inhabited by their internal counterparts.

It is interesting to compare the nondualistic worldview of the nineteenth-century Tibetan contemplative Düdjom Lingpa to the dualistic European worldview of the sixteenth and seventeenth centuries. These were the formative years of the Scientific Revolution and the Protestant Reformation, both of which arose when Europe was engaged in a pathological struggle with demons and witches. In the European worldview of that era, demons were real, they were external, and they wreaked havoc in the lives of individuals and in society. Demons also posed a problem for natural philosophers, the men who later came to be known as *scientists*, who were trying to understand the mechanisms and natural laws of the physical universe.

Isaac Newton came up with a solution to the problem of demons by confining them to the subjective realm of the human mind. By sweeping the external world clean of demons, he made the physical world a more predictable and safe place for scientific inquiry. Newton siphoned the demons of the Western world into the repository of the human mind, leaving the objective world of space, time, and matter saturated by the light of God's infinite love and intelligence. From a Buddhist perspective, this may be construed as Newton's own version of *tonglen*. But rather than extinguishing those demons in the light of one's heart, Newton let them remain in the human mind, where they lurked in silence until Freud started poking into the recesses of the psyche two hundred years later.

Buddhism acknowledges that demons exist, but they are neither absolutely objective nor absolutely subjective. They arise within the realm of human experience in which all appearances—objective and subjective— present themselves to us. When you plumb through the strata of the psyche by such practices as settling the mind in its natural state, you may encounter phenomena that appear as demons. It is crucial to understand that demons can appear to your mind as a result of *correct* practice, let alone misguided practice. If you are Tibetan, the demons you encounter may have multiple heads and arms. If you are a Westerner, your demons may arise in forms more widely accepted within our society. As you dredge the depths of your psyche, your own demons will emerge into the light of your consciousness. You can count on it.

Düdjom Lingpa's explanation of demons is that they are externalized projections of afflictive tendencies of the mind, such as hatred, greed, confusion, pride, and jealousy. When demons arise, there is a natural tendency among Tibetans, even experienced practitioners, to go to a doctor and report what is happening in meditation. When the medicine from the doctor changes nothing, the next trip might be to an astrologer. If astrology fails, the next visit might be to a psychic. However, if the reason demons arise is that one is not housecleaning a neurotic mind, all the external efforts to get rid of them won't help. We have to work through the problems. How do we do that? Let it rise, and let it pass. Let the demons of the mind reveal themselves and instead of clinging to them or grappling with them, allow them to vanish of their own accord back into the luminous space of awareness. This is the practice of allowing the mind to heal itself.

In *The Vajra Essence*, Düdjom Lingpa claims that all such beings have no existence except as appearances to the mind. While this is the view of many psychologists today, it is important to recognize that he also asserts that the self is no more real than these other apparitions to the mind. Both are "empty" of inherent, objective existence, and we, not some imaginary, supernatural beings, are responsible for what befalls us. Many Buddhist meditation manuals present normative accounts of what to expect in meditative practice when it is done properly. Such texts are valuable, but they don't give a clear account of the many challenges that arise as a result of proper practice. Most manuals tell you what *should* happen, not what often *does* happen even when practice is done correctly and consistently.

In contrast, *The Vajra Essence* provides at the beginning of its presentation of the entire path to enlightenment an account of a wide array of meditative experiences (Tibetan: *nyam*) that may occur on the path of shamatha. The specific shamatha practice he emphasizes as a preparation for Dzogchen is settling the mind in its natural state, which he calls "taking the mind and its appearances as the object of meditation."

The Vajra Essence emphasizes above all that there is no consistency in the specific experiences from one individual to the next. Everyone's mind is so unimaginably complex that there is no way to predict with confidence the types of experiences each person will experience. Here is a list of just some of the kinds of meditative experiences cited in this text that may arise during this training, especially when it is pursued in solitude for many hours each day, for months on end:[57]

- The impression that all your thoughts are wreaking havoc in your body and mind, like boulders rolling down a steep mountain, crushing and destroying everything in their path
- A sharp pain in your heart as a result of all your thoughts, as if you had been pierced with the tip of a sword
- The ecstatic, blissful sense that mental stillness is pleasurable, but movement is painful
- The perception of all phenomena as brilliant, colored particles
- Intolerable pain throughout your body from the tips of the hair on your head down to the tips of your toenails
- The sense that even food and drink are harmful due to your being afflicted by a variety of physical disorders
- An inexplicable sense of paranoia about meeting other people, visiting their homes, or being in public places
- Compulsive hope in medical treatment, divinations, and astrology
- Such unbearable misery that you think your heart will burst

- Insomnia at night, or fitful sleep like that of someone who is critically ill
- Grief and disorientation when you wake up
- The conviction that there is still some decisive understanding or knowledge that you must have, and yearning for it like a thirsty person longing for water
- The emergence, one after another, of all kinds of afflictive thoughts, and being impelled to pursue them, as painful as that may be
- Various speech impediments and respiratory ailments
- The conviction that there is some special meaning in every external sound that you hear and form that you see, and thinking, "That must be a sign or omen for me," compulsively speculating about the chirping of birds and everything else you see and feel
- The sensation of external sounds and voices of humans, dogs, birds, and so on all piercing your heart like thorns
- Unbearable anger due to the paranoia of thinking that everyone else is gossiping about you and putting you down
- Negative reactions when you hear and see others joking around and laughing, thinking that they are making fun of you, and retaliating verbally
- Because of your own experience of suffering, compulsive longing for others' happiness when you watch them
- Fear and terror about weapons and even your own friends because your mind is filled with a constant stream of anxieties
- Everything around you leading to all kinds of hopes and fears
- When you get into bed at night, premonitions of others who will come the next day
- Uncontrollable fear, anger, obsessive attachment, and hatred when images arise, seeing others' faces, forms, minds, and conversations, as well as demons and so forth, preventing you from falling asleep
- Weeping out of reverence and devotion to your gurus, your faith and devotion in the objects of religious devotion, your sense of renunciation and disillusionment with the cycle of existence, and your heartfelt compassion for sentient beings

- Rough experiences, followed by the disappearance of all your suffering and the saturation of your mind with radiant clarity and ecstasy, like pristine space
- The experience that gods or demons are actually carrying away your head, limbs, and vital organs, leaving behind only a vapor trail; or merely having the sensation of this happening, or it occurring in a dream
- A sense of ecstasy as if a stormy sky had become free of clouds

While many of us would likely respond to some of those disagreeable experiences by stopping the practice or seeking medical help, Düdjom Lingpa actually called them all "signs of progress"! It truly is progress when you recognize how cluttered and turbulent your mind is. But the deeper you venture into the inner wilderness of the mind, the more you encounter all kinds of unexpected and, at times, deeply troubling memories and impulses that manifest both psychologically and physically. At times, these may become so disturbing that psychological counseling or medical treatment may be necessary. Düdjom Lingpa's advice is to stay a steady course in the practice, continuing to observe whatever comes up, without distraction and without grasping. This is a tall order, but it is the way forward. There is no way to probe the depths of consciousness except by way of the psyche, with all its neuroses and imbalances. It should come as some solace that none of these unnerving experiences are freshly introduced into your mind by meditative practice. Whatever comes up was already there, previously hidden by the turbulence and dullness of the mind.

While Düdjom Lingpa emphasized how utterly unpredictable these meditative experiences are, he did comment on some general tendencies corresponding to individuals with the different psychophysical constitutions related to the five elements:[58]

> For a person with a fire constitution, a sense of joy is prominent;
> for one with an earth constitution, a sense of dullness is prominent; for one with a water constitution, a sense of clarity is prominent; for one with an air constitution, harsh sensations are

prominent; and for one with a space constitution, a sense of vacuity is prominent.

In Tibetan Buddhism, which is closely associated with traditional Tibetan medicine, the human body, like the physical environment, is composed of five elements. Most people are dominant in one or more elements, and this influences their physical constitution, behavior, and mental traits. Here is a brief synopsis of these five types of constitution:[59]

Earth constitution

Positive aspects: feelings of being stable, grounded, and confident; one's confidence and aspirations are steady, as is one's sense of responsibility

Negative aspects: qualities of dullness, laziness, and inertia; one's thinking may be heavy, literal, and lacking creativity; apathy and depression; insensitive and uninspired

Water constitution

Positive aspects: comfort in oneself and one's life; fluid, easily navigating one's way through life; accepting of conditions, joyful and content

Negative aspects: complacency, lacking in productivity, a weak and drifting mind; highly emotional and oversensitive

Fire constitution

Positive aspects: the capacity to initiate projects and carry them through to completion; intuition and enthusiasm, inspired undertakings, joy in one's work and accomplishments

Negative aspects: easily agitated, irritable, impetuous, unstable, restless, intolerant, garrulous, insomniac

Air constitution

Positive aspects: the ability to change negative situations into positive ones; curiosity, flexibility of intellect

Negative aspects: little stability or contentment; fickle, difficulty in accepting things as they are, jittery, unfocused, anxious, flighty; emotionally unstable

Space constitution

Positive aspects: ability to accommodate to whatever life brings; tolerance and balance in all things

Negative aspects: spacey, loss of connection with what's happening; loss of meaning through a superficial connection with life; lack of awareness, being out of touch

It should come as some consolation that the difficulties encountered in the practice of settling the mind in its natural state are finite. Eventually you will emerge through the layers of the psyche into a clear and luminous space of awareness. Düdjom Lingpa describes this breakthrough as follows:

> After all pleasant and harsh sensations have disappeared into the space of the mind, by just letting thoughts be, without having to do anything with them, all appearances lose their capacity to help or harm, and you can remain in that state. You may also have an extraordinary sense of joy, luminosity, and nonconceptuality.[60]

While the terms "joy" and "luminosity" are familiar in common English usage, and "nonconceptuality" is the absence of something with which we are all familiar, what these terms actually mean at this advanced stage of meditation cannot be imagined unless you have reached that stage yourself. This is where language can be misleading. Words used to describe such states of consciousness must give some idea to nonmeditators and novices of what takes place when high degrees of attentional balance are achieved. But it is a great mistake to assume that just because one has a layperson's knowledge of the meaning of these terms that one has understood what they mean in these rarified contexts.

LUCID DREAMING—
DAYTIME PRACTICE

I n the Buddhist tradition, the primary purpose of developing shamatha is
to apply the enhanced stability and vividness of attention to experiential
inquiry into the nature of reality. The term *buddha* literally means "one
who is awake," and the implication here is that the rest of us are compar-
atively asleep, moving through life as if in a dream. When you're dreaming and don't know it, that's called a *nonlucid dream*, but when you recognize
that you're dreaming in the midst of the dream, this is called a *lucid dream*.
The overall aim of Buddhist insight practice is to "wake up" to all states of
consciousness, both during the daytime and nighttime, to become lucid at
all times.

Over the past thirty years, lucid dreaming has become a subject of scientific research, and effective means have been developed to recognize the
dream state while it is occurring.[61] Between your sessions of shamatha meditation, you may find it helpful to begin engaging in some of these practices
as you begin to apply your focused attention to the cultivation of insight.

You may start your practice of *daytime lucid dreaming* by mindfully attending to the way you actually perceive the physical world of your body and
environment. Many of us believe that we directly perceive objective, physical phenomena with our five physical senses, that the mental images we
perceive via our senses are accurate representations of the objects we perceive. However, neurologist Antonio Damasio refutes this assumption,
which is commonly called *naïve realism*:[62]

The problem with the term *representation* is not its ambiguity, since everyone can guess what it means, but the implication that, somehow, the mental image or the neural pattern *represents*, in mind and in brain, with some degree of fidelity, the object to which the representation refers, as if the structure of the object were replicated in the representation.... When you and I look at an object outside ourselves, we form comparable images in our respective brains. We know this well because you and I can describe the object in very similar ways, down to fine details. But that does not mean that the image we see is the copy of whatever the object outside is like. Whatever it is like, in absolute terms, we do not know.

In light of this neuroscientific view, with our five senses we directly perceive images generated in the brain, but these are not truly representations of anything existing independently of the brain. These sensory impressions of colors, sounds, smells, and so on are no more tangible than thoughts or dreams. While we seem to experience colors and so on as they exist in the objective world, independent of our senses, this is an illusion, very much like a dream.

We may conclude from this that the only realities we directly perceive consist of appearances to the mind and the five senses, none of which are demonstrably physical. There's no objective "yardstick" by which to compare our sensory perceptions or concepts with the physical phenomena "out there" that we imagine exist independently of our perceptions and concepts. The very existence of an independently existing universe made up of phenomena we have defined as physical now seems to be called into question. And our normal waking experience takes on a dreamlike quality.

These comments closely parallel the philosopher Immanuel Kant's thinking, and the implication here is not that there's no universe independent of the human mind (physical or otherwise), but rather, as Kant argued, as soon as we try to perceive it or conceive of it, we do so by means of our human sensory and cognitive faculties, none of which provide us with access to reality as it exists independent of our modes of inquiry. This same point was made by the physicist Werner Heisenberg: "What we observe is not nature in itself but nature exposed to our method of questioning."[63]

While scientists since the time of Galileo have tried to fathom the nature of objective reality, existing independently of human experience, Buddhists have sought to understand what they called *loka*, comparable to what the phenomenologists call the *Lebenswelt*, the world of experience. Like a dream, the world of waking experience does not exist independently of our experience of it. The daytime practices in preparation for lucid nighttime dreaming may help begin to wake you up to the nature of your experienced world. The most effective method of learning to achieve lucidity is to develop a "critical-reflective attitude" toward your state of consciousness by asking yourself whether or not you are dreaming while you are awake.

"WAKING UP" THROUGHOUT THE DAY

The lucid dreaming daytime practices consist of (1) doing "state checks," (2) checking for dreamsigns, and (3) anticipating dreaming lucidly at night.

State Checks

A *state check* enables you to determine whether, right now, you are awake or dreaming. During the waking state, the physical world you experience is not entirely dependent on your own mind. For example, as you read the pages of this book, although the visual images you are seeing are produced by your brain, the paper and ink were produced by other people and consist of chemical substances that do not depend for their existence on your perception of them. If you momentarily turn your head away from the book, the paper and ink still exist, although your visual appearances of them don't. Given the independent status of the book relative to your perception of it, every time you look back to the lines of text on this page, you see the same words. On the other hand, if you were dreaming right now, the book you are reading would have no existence apart from your perception of it. It would be purely a creation of your own mind, so if you momentarily close your eyes or turn your head away, that dreamed book wouldn't exist at all. Being out of sight, it would be out of mind and cease to exist. Given the lack of continuity of any objective book in a dream, when you redirect your gaze back to the book, the words change seventy-five percent of the time if you reread it once, and ninety-five percent of the time if you reread it twice.

So try this right now. Turn your head away for a few seconds, then look at this page again. If the words change (and of course you would need to remember what they were previously to know that), then you are almost certainly dreaming. If they remain the same, you are probably awake. If you do this a second and even a third time, and the words still remain the same, then you can conclude with greater and greater certainty that you are not dreaming. But if they change even once, then you are probably correct to conclude that you are dreaming.

This exercise may seem silly since you presumably were already quite confident that you weren't dreaming. But we commonly have that same confidence when we are dreaming. We take what we experience in the world around us to be objectively real, existing independently of our aware-ness of it, and we respond to events as if we were awake. By conducting state checks intermittently throughout the course of the day, you can deter-mine whether you are awake or asleep. And as you familiarize yourself with this practice, this habit may carry over into your dream state, and when you apply it then, you will suddenly discover that you *are* dreaming. This is how you begin to dream lucidly.

In the practice of shamatha you develop *present memory*, as in the case of remembering to focus your attention on your chosen object in the ongo-ing flow of the present moment. You also recall prospectively how to rec-ognize attentional imbalances and remedy them when either laxity or excitation arises. In a similar way, the daytime practice of lucid dreaming includes *prospectively remembering* to conduct state checks throughout the day. Also, if you at any time experience an exceptionally odd situation, pause and ask yourself, "How odd is it?" While dreaming, we experience many anomalies, such as abrupt transitions of our location and other kinds of dis-continuities, such as the words in a book changing, or other weird occur-rences and circumstances. But without adopting a "critical-reflective attitude" toward them, we take them in stride, without waking up to the fact that we are dreaming. Adopt such a critical stance at all times, questioning the nature of your present experience; this habit, too, may carry over into the dream state and help you to become lucid.

Dreamsigns

Dreamsigns are out-of-the-ordinary events that often occur in dreams and that, when you notice them, may indicate to you that you are dreaming. In this practice, you monitor your experience for the appearance of dream-signs, of which there are three types.

Individual dreamsigns consist of activities, situations, people, objects, and mental states that you commonly experience in your dreams. In order to identify and watch for these dreamsigns, you will need to pay close attention to your dreams and keep a dream journal, noting the circum-stances that are recurrent. Remember these and whenever you experience them, pause for a moment and conduct a state check to see if you might be dreaming.

Strong dreamsigns consist of events that, as far as you know, can happen only in a dream. For example, if you are reading a book and it turns into a squid, that's a strong dreamsign, and if you recognize it as such, you've become lucid. Many other "supernatural events" commonly occur in dreams, but if you fail to apply a critical-reflective attitude to these strong dreamsigns, you will continue to take everything you experience as being objectively real.

Weak dreamsigns are events that are highly improbable but not completely impossible as far as you know. Seeing an elephant sauntering across your front lawn is one example of a weak dreamsign unless you live in the jun-gles of Sri Lanka or on a game reservation in Kenya. When you experience anything that's a bit out of the ordinary, conduct a state check. If there's something in sight that you can read, conduct the previous state check. If there's nothing of the sort, you can simply take a close look at your sur-roundings and see whether they are as stable as your normal waking expe-rience. Look out for inexplicable fluctuations that may indicate a dream.

Anticipation

Throughout the course of the day, recall that tonight you will sleep and dream, and repeatedly arouse the strong resolution, "Tonight when I'm dreaming, I will recognize the dream state for what it is." The stability and vividness of attention that you have cultivated in your shamatha practice, together with the exercise of prospective memory, should serve you well now and bring clarity to all your experiences, both waking and dreaming.

STAGE 7: FULLY PACIFIED ATTENTION ● ● ●

Once you have met the challenges of the first six stages of attentional development, you ascend to the seventh, which is called *fully pacified attention*. Asanga succinctly characterizes this stage of development with the statement, "Attachment, melancholy, and so on are pacified as they arise."[64] Such experiences may continue to occur from time to time, but they have lost their power to disturb the equilibrium of your mind. Involuntary thoughts continue to course through the mind like a river slowly flowing through a valley, but as your mind settles more and more deeply in its natural state, there is nothing for them to attach to. In the absence of grasping, you are not attached to them, and they have no power in themselves to afflict you.

The power by which the seventh stage is achieved is *enthusiasm*: the practice itself now fills you with joy. It is this that motivates you to continue in the practice, meeting the increasingly subtle challenges ahead. Having overcome the medium degree of laxity, subtle laxity remains, in which the object of mindfulness appears vividly, but your attention is slightly slack. No one but a highly advanced meditator is even capable of recognizing such a subtle degree of laxity. It is detected only in relation to the exceptionally high degree of vividness of which the trained mind is capable. Subtle excitation also occurs from time to time. As recommended previously, when laxity sets in, you arouse your attention; and when excitation occurs, you loosen up slightly. At the seventh stage, these subtle attentional imbalances are swiftly recognized due to your finely honed faculty of introspection, and they are easily remedied. The Tibetan word *gom,* usually translated as "meditation," has the connotation of *familiarity*, and that is the quality of your experience at the stage of fully pacified attention. You have become highly adept at balancing and refining your attention, and the rest of the journey to the realization of shamatha is all downhill.

Upon reaching the seventh stage of fully pacified attention, the mind has been so refined that your meditation sessions may last for at least two hours with only the slightest interruptions by laxity and excitation. In each of the two shamatha methods introduced thus far—mindfulness of breathing and settling the mind in its natural state—the practices gradually involve doing less and less. When mindfully attending to the breath, there is a great deal you are not doing, but you are still releasing involuntary thoughts when they arise. You do prefer to have a conceptually silent mind, as opposed to having discursive thoughts and images arise one after the other. When settling the mind in its natural state, you are doing even less. Now you don't even prefer thoughts to be absent. Instead of deliberately letting them go—banishing them from your mind—you let them be, without deliberately influencing them in any way. You simply maintain constant mindfulness of the space of the mind and whatever events occur in that space.

THE PRACTICE: SETTLING THE MIND IN ITS NATURAL STATE— OBSERVING THE MOVEMENT OF THE MIND

The First Panchen Lama called this practice *meditation on the relative nature of the mind*,[65] and Düdjom Lingpa called it *taking appearances and awareness as the path*.[66] The First Panchen Lama describes this practice as follows:

> Whatever sort of thoughts arise, without suppressing them, recognize where they are moving and where they are moving to; and focus while observing the nature of those thoughts. By so doing, eventually their movement ceases and there is stillness. This is like the example of the flight over the ocean of an uncaged bird that has long been kept onboard a ship at sea. Practice in accord with the description in [Saraha's] *Song of Realization*:

"Like a raven that flies from a ship, circles around in all directions, and alights there again."[67]

In ancient times, when Indian mariners sailed far out to sea, they would release a caged raven they had brought onboard and observe its flight. After flying around higher and higher in ever-widening circles, if the raven flew off in one direction, the navigator would know that was the direction of the nearest land. But if there was no land in sight for the raven, as much as it might wish to alight elsewhere, since it could not swim it had no choice but to return to the ship. Likewise, when thoughts arise, let them play out their course, regardless of their nature or duration. In the end, they can only disappear back into the space of awareness from which they initially arose. In this practice it is crucial to observe the movement of thoughts without intervention. This is a vital aspect to the natural healing of the mind that takes place in this process.

REFLECTIONS ON THE PRACTICE

Mindfulness and Contemplative Insight

The practice of settling the mind in its natural state corresponds closely to the psychological description of mindfulness, explained earlier as "a kind of nonelaborative, nonjudgmental, present-centered awareness in which each thought, feeling, or sensation that arises in the attentional field is acknowledged and accepted as it is."[68] This description, as discussed in chapter 4, reflects the contemporary Vipassana tradition's account of mindfulness as a kind of moment-to-moment "bare attention" or nonconceptual awareness that does not label or categorize experiences. Indian and Tibetan Buddhist contemplatives, however, regard the practice of settling the mind in its natural state as a specific technique for developing shamatha, not contemplative insight, or *vipashyana*.

Bhante Gunaratana, speaking for the contemporary Vipassana tradition, states that *samadhi*, or concentration, "could be defined as that faculty of the mind which focuses single-pointedly on one object without interruption." And he describes mindfulness as the faculty that "notices that...distraction has occurred, and it is mindfulness which redirects the attention."[69] Thus, for Gunaratana, concentration performs the function that we have been calling mindfulness, and mindfulness as he describes it performs the function that we have been calling introspection. It may be helpful to note these terminological differences from one tradition to another, without getting hung up on them. However, it is also worth noting that according to the classic texts cited here, the shamatha practice of bare attention applied to the domain of the mind results only in the temporary alleviation of such mental afflictions as craving and hostility. So there's no reason to believe that the practice of bare attention alone will irreversibly dispel any affliction of the mind.

According to Buddhist tradition, such liberation is achieved through the practice of *vipashyana*, or insight meditation, which results in wisdom. Such realization, when fused with the exceptional attentional stability and clarity of shamatha, irreversibly eliminates the ignorance and delusion that lie at the root of suffering. On the other hand, if our practice of vipashyana is not supported by the achievement of shamatha, no realization, awakening, or transformation will last, and we will never rise above the wounds of our human pain. The liberation that results from the unification of shamatha and vipashyana in no way places us outside the reality of change. The Buddha, too, grew old and died. But the freedom gained by the Buddha and all those who have followed his path to liberation to its culmination has irrevocably healed their minds from craving, hostility, and delusion and their resultant suffering. Anything less is unworthy of the name "nirvana."

Within the Buddhist noble eightfold path, right effort, right concentration, and right mindfulness are ancillary to cultivation of samadhi. Right thought and right view are the essential elements of the eightfold path needed for the cultivation of wisdom. This further indicates that mindfulness alone is insufficient for liberating the mind completely from its afflictive tendencies. To achieve the insight that results in true freedom, one must exercise great clarity of thought, making use of views like the Buddhist ones much as a scientist uses working hypotheses in conducting experiments. The practice of meditation that is unrelated to any view or hypothesis is as limited as scientific research that is conducted without reference to a scientific view of reality.

Exploring the Relative Ground State of Consciousness

According to the Mahayana tradition, the practice of settling the mind in its natural state leads to a realization of the *relative* nature of consciousness and the *temporary* alleviation of certain hindrances, or obscurations, of the mind. This is why the First Panchen Lama called it *meditation on the conventional nature of the mind* and cautioned that many contemplatives in Tibet had mistaken meditative experiences from this practice for realization of ultimate truth.

Both the Theravada and the Indo-Tibetan traditions of Buddhism agree that the cultivation of shamatha leads to an experiential realization of the ground state of the psyche. Early Buddhist literature refers to this as the bhavanga, literally, "the ground of becoming," which supports all kinds of mental activities and sensory perceptions, as the root of a tree sustains the trunk, branches, and leaves. The bhavanga may be characterized as a relative vacuum state of consciousness, voided of all the "kinetic energy" of active thoughts, mental imagery, and sense perceptions. Generally speaking, it is indiscernible while the mind is active, for it normally manifests only in dreamless sleep and during the very last moment of a person's life. While it is depicted as the natural, unencumbered state of the mind, its innate radiance and purity are present even when the mind is obscured by afflictive thoughts and emotions.[70] In contrast to the materialistic view of the mind, Buddhist contemplatives assert that all mental and sensory processes are conditioned by the body and the environment, but they actually emerge from the bhavanga, not the brain.

Theravada commentators insist that the bhavanga is an *intermittent* phase of consciousness, which is interrupted whenever sensory consciousness or other kinds of cognitive activity arise. So it is not an ongoing repository of memories or any other mental imprints. Despite the fact that the bhavanga is described as the naturally pure and radiant state of awareness that exists whether or not the mind is obscured with defilements, this school—perhaps out of a concern that it be seen as a permanent, independent Self—denies that it is an ever-present substrate.

I believe Dzogchen contemplatives who have achieved shamatha gain access to this same dimension of consciousness, but they interpret it in a somewhat different way. The *substrate consciousness (alayavijñana)*, as they call it, consists of a stream of arising and passing moments of consciousness, so it is not permanent; and it is conditioned by various influences, so it is not independent. But they do regard it as a continuous stream of consciousness from which all mundane cognitive processes arise.

In the natural course of a life, the substrate consciousness is repeatedly experienced in dreamless sleep, and it finally manifests at the moment of death. A contemplative may consciously probe this dimension of consciousness through the practice of shamatha, in which discursive thoughts become dormant and all appearances of oneself, others, one's body, and one's environment vanish. At this point, as in the cases of sleeping and dying, the mind is drawn inward and the physical senses become dormant. What remains is a state of radiant, clear consciousness that is the basis for the emergence of all appearances to an individual's mindstream. All phenomena appearing to sensory and mental perception are imbued with the clarity of this substrate consciousness. Like the reflections of the planets and stars in a pool of limpid, clear water, so do the appearances of the entire phenomenal world appear within this empty, clear substrate consciousness.

The substrate consciousness may be characterized as the relative ground state of the individual mind, in the sense that it entails the lowest state of activity, with the highest potential and degree of freedom that can be achieved by evacuating the mind through the practice of samadhi. For example, once an individual stream of consciousness has been catalyzed from its own substrate in dreamless sleep, it can freely manifest in a vast diversity of dreamscapes and experiences. Such exceptional creativity also is displayed while under deep hypnosis, which also taps into the substrate consciousness. But this potential is most effectively accessed when one lucidly penetrates to the substrate consciousness by means of meditative quiescence. In this case, one is vividly aware of the substrate, in contrast to the dullness that normally characterizes dreamless sleep. Buddhist contemplatives report that such fully conscious realization of the ground state of consciousness opens up a tremendous wellspring of creativity, which is largely obscured in the normal experiences of the substrate while sleeping or dying.

Contemplatives who have realized the substrate consciousness through the practice of shamatha claim that it is imbued with three attributes: bliss, luminosity, and nonconceptuality. These have led many contemplatives to mistake the substrate consciousness for the ultimate nature of reality, or nirvana. But simply dwelling in this relative vacuum state of consciousness does not liberate the mind of its afflictive tendencies or their resultant suffering. By fathoming the nature of the substrate consciousness, one comes to know the nature of consciousness in its relative ground state. This realization, however, does not illuminate the nature of reality as a whole. It is also important not to confuse this substrate consciousness with a collective unconscious, as conceived by Carl Jung. Buddhist accounts of the substrate consciousness all refer to it as an *individual* stream of consciousness that carries on from one lifetime to the next.

The Dzogchen tradition draws a distinction between the substrate consciousness and the substrate (*alaya*), which is described as the objective, empty space of the mind. This vacuum state is immaterial like space, a blank, unthinking void into which all objective appearances of the physical senses and mental perception dissolve when one falls asleep; and it is out of this vacuum that appearances reemerge upon waking.[71]

At this point in the practice of shamatha, you will have honed your ability to attend to all kinds of mental processes without distraction and without grasping. Even when the mental toxins of craving, anger, and delusion arise, you will be able to observe them without being sucked into them. And insofar as you don't grasp onto them or identify with them, they become detoxified and can no longer disturb the equilibrium of your mind. To the extent that you are able to release these mental processes into their natural state, they are no longer even experienced as mental afflictions, and you may now begin to explore their more essential nature.

When you experience craving, you may notice the bliss that arises in the anticipation of joy and satisfaction. You are seeing through the afflictions of your psyche and sensing the bliss that is a quality of your substrate consciousness. At all times, when craving arises for anything such as possessions, notoriety, sensual enjoyments, or even for the accomplishment of shamatha, you can attend to the bliss in the craving.

In the heat of anger you may discover luminosity, a second quality of the substrate consciousness. Whenever anger blazes up, you have the opportunity not to be carried away by nor identify with it. Instead, you may attend closely to the luminosity that is manifesting as anger and begin to fathom the deeper nature of consciousness.

Even in delusion there is an aspect of the substrate consciousness: nonconceptuality. So whenever you experience delusion, attend to its deeper, unafflictive nature of nonconceptuality. By carefully attending to the mind with discerning awareness, we can begin to experience three qualities of the substrate consciousness—bliss, luminosity, and nonconceptuality—as they manifest as anger, craving, and delusion. When you are carried away by or identify with these mental processes, they disrupt the equilibrium of the mind and lead to harmful behavior. But when you attend to them without distraction and without grasping, they become portals to the primary characteristics of the substrate consciousness.

As you continue to develop the stability and vividness of your attention throughout the daytime, you may want to apply these qualities to illuminate the nature of your nighttime experiences as well. After all, most of us spend up to a third of our lives sleeping. With the refinement of attention you have now attained, you are well prepared to enfold the sleeping portion of your life in your meditative practice. As you venture into the nighttime practice of lucid dreaming, you can begin to explore the similarities and differences between waking and dreaming states of consciousness. Stephen LaBerge, a prominent researcher in this field, comments, "Dreaming can be viewed as the special case of perception without the constraints of external sensory input. Conversely, perception can be viewed as the special case of dreaming constrained by sensory input."[72] The only essential difference between waking and dreaming experiences is that the former arise with sensory input and the latter without it. In terms of the activity in our brains, dreaming of perceiving or doing something closely parallels perceiving or doing it in the waking state. This, LaBerge comments, is why we regularly mistake our dreams for reality.[73]

There are three essential requirements for learning lucid dreaming: adequate motivation, correct practice of effective techniques, and excellent dream recall. You can develop an adequate motivation by reflecting on the potential benefits of such practice for fathoming the nature of consciousness, and you can develop excellent dream recall by paying close attention to your dreams and recording them in a journal. In his most recent book on lucid dreaming, *Lucid Dreaming: A Concise Guide to Awakening in Your Dreams and in Your Life,* LaBerge provides detailed, practical instructions on this practice, which I shall briefly summarize here.

One technique that directly builds on the daytime practices discussed in the previous interlude is called the Mnemonic Induction of Lucid Dreams (MILD). In this practice, as you go to bed at night, you resolve to wake up and recall your dreams throughout the night. As soon as you awaken from the dream, you try to recall as many details as possible from the dream, and when you are about to fall back asleep, you focus your mind on the resolve, "The next time I dream, I shall recognize it as a dream!" And just before you doze off, imagine that you are back in the dream from which you just awakened.

Dream-Initiated Lucid Dreams (DILD) occur when you somehow realize that you are dreaming while in the midst of an ongoing dream. This recognition may occur because you have identified a strong or weak dream-sign, or it may be catalyzed by a nightmare. This is the most common way to become lucid in a dream.

In Wake-Initiated Lucid Dreams (WILD) you briefly awaken from a dream, then return right back to it without losing consciousness. LaBerge describes this practice as follows:

> You lie in bed deeply relaxed but vigilant, and perform a repetitive or continuous mental activity upon which you focus your attention. Keeping this task going is what maintains your inner focus of attention and with it your wakeful inner consciousness, while your drowsy external awareness diminishes and finally vanishes altogether as you fall asleep. In essence, the idea is to let your body fall asleep while you keep your mind awake.[74]

Many people find the prospect of lucid dreaming daunting because they have a hard time recalling their dreams, or even when they do, the dreams themselves may be unclear and their recollection of them may be vague. These are problems of attentional laxity, which are directly remedied through the practice of shamatha. Another problem often encountered when first venturing into the practices of lucid dreaming is waking up as soon as you recognize that you are dreaming. Even if you don't wake up, the dream may fade out and your lucidity may go with it. Or the dream may continue, but you may lose your awareness that it is a dream. These problems stem from insufficient attentional stability, which shamatha is also designed to develop. So shamatha appears to be perfectly designed to provide you with just those qualities of attention needed to become adept at lucid dreaming.

A major cause of forgetting dreams is interference from other mental contents competing for your attention, so let the first thought upon awakening be "What was I just dreaming?" Just as movement disrupts attentional stability while meditating, it also undermines the coherence and continuity of dreaming, so do not move when you first wake up. Redirect your attention to the dream from which you just awoke, and see if you can slip right back into it, mindfully aware that it is a dream.

Another very effective way to become proficient in lucid dreaming is to wake up one hour earlier than usual, and stay awake for thirty to sixty minutes before going back to sleep. This can increase the likelihood of having a lucid dream by as much as twenty times. As you become more and more adept at maintaining the stability and vividness of your attention at all times, during and between meditation sessions, while awake and asleep, you will gain deeper and deeper insight into the nature of awareness as you progress along the path of shamatha.

THE ADVANCED STAGES:
ILLUMINATING AWARENESS

STAGE 8: SINGLE-POINTED ATTENTION ● ● ●

By continuing in the sustained cultivation of shamatha, eventually you will achieve the eighth stage, known as *single-pointed attention*. You have now realized a high degree of unification of attention: wherever you direct it, your awareness is coherent and highly focused. From this point onward, you can flow with the momentum of the practice with little or no effort. You can now sustain a high level of *samadhi*, or highly focused attention, free of the imbalances of even the subtlest laxity and excitation for at least three hours or so. Only the slightest degree of effort at the beginning of each session is need to ward off these obstacles, and you continue in your practice motivated by the power of enthusiasm. For the first time, the flow of attention proceeds without any interruptions by laxity or excitation, and the overall quality of this state of samadhi is one of stillness. Whereas in the preceding stages, involuntary thoughts arose like a river slowly flowing through a valley, now the mind feels calm, like an ocean unmoved by waves.

If you wish to continue in settling the mind in its natural state, this practice can take you all the way to the achievement of shamatha. But I shall now present an alternative practice that you may find an even more potent way to balance your attention to perfection. Padmasambhava calls this technique the cultivation of *shamatha without a sign*. In this context, the term *sign* refers to any object of attention that can be identified within a conceptual framework. The tactile sensations of the breath are a sign. So is the space of the mind and the mental events that arise within that space. In both those practices, the attention is directed to an object other than itself, and stability and vividness are cultivated in relation to that object.

✓ In the practice of shamatha without a sign, the attention is not directed *to* anything. It rests in its own nature, simply being aware of its own presence. Nominally, you could say that awareness takes itself as its object. But experientially, this practice is more a matter of taking no object. You simply let your awareness rest, without any referent, in its own innate luminosity and cognizance. While Padmasambhava presents this as a method for achieving shamatha, it is also an effective method for illuminating the nature of awareness itself.

We know—or at least *think* we know—many things about our physical environment, other people, our bodies, our minds, and ourselves. But as scientists have repeatedly found over the past four centuries, many things of which we believe we have certain knowledge turn out to be illusory. Of what can we be absolutely certain? Very few scientists would claim such certitude about even their most rigorously tested findings. As Descartes and many other philosophers in the East and West have noted, the very existence of an independent, objective, physical world may be called into question. Perhaps it, too, is an illusion. This is the basic premise of philosophical idealism. On the other hand, many materialists claim that all our subjective mental experiences are illusory, and most cognitive scientists have concluded that our normal sense of an autonomous self is an illusion. But in the midst of all these uncertainties, I propose there is one kind of knowledge of which we can be absolutely certain: our knowledge of the presence of consciousness. Even if we are not sure there is a distinct observer—the self—it is unreasonable to doubt that conscious experience takes place. Without it, it would be impossible to doubt its existence.

This is a more modest claim than Descartes' famous dictum, "I think, therefore I am." Thoughts occur, but that doesn't necessarily imply there is a separate agent called *I*. Moreover, as you discover in the cultivation of shamatha, there are times when thoughts are absent. But there can still be an awareness of that absence, with or without a separate observer who is conscious of that absence. It is also possible to be aware of being aware. Imagine the thought experiment of immersing yourself in a sensory deprivation tank that is so effective that you lose all sensory awareness of your body and physical environment. All you are left with is the space of your mind and the thoughts, images, desires, emotions, and so forth arising in that space. Now imagine that this space of awareness is voided of all contents. Even without a sign—an object that you can identify conceptually and to which you can direct your attention—there can still be an awareness of the sheer luminosity and cognizance of being aware. The mind has been reduced to its bare nature, a relative vacuum state. But that emptiness is still illuminated by consciousness. And this awareness is innate, still, and vivid. The qualities of attention you have earlier been developing through the practices of shamatha are already implicit in the nature of awareness itself. They have just been waiting to be unveiled.

THE PRACTICE: AWARENESS OF AWARENESS

After settling your body and mind in their natural states, you can simply be aware of being aware. You don't need to be in a sensory deprivation tank, and your mind doesn't have to be totally silenced. You can know, with immediate certainty, that consciousness is present, and with no other object of awareness, you can cultivate attentional stability and vividness of that awareness. Let's see how Padmasambhava describes this subtlest way of achieving shamatha:

> While steadily gazing into the space in front of you, without meditating on anything, steadily concentrate your consciousness, without wavering, in the space in front of you. Increase the stability of attention and then relax again. Occasionally seek out: "What is that consciousness that is concentrating?" Steadily concentrate again, and then check it out again. Do that in an alternating fashion. Even if there are problems of laxity and lethargy, that will dispel them....
>
> Cast your gaze downwards, gently release your mind, and without having anything on which to meditate, gently release both your body and mind into their natural state. Having nothing on which to meditate, and without any modification or adulteration,

rest your attention simply without wavering, in its own natural state, its natural limpidity, its own character, just as it is. Remain in that state of luminosity, and rest your mind so that it is loose and free. Alternate between observing that which is concentrating inwardly and that which is releasing. If you think it is the mind, ask: "Who is it that releases the mind and concentrates the mind?" Steadily observe yourself, then release again. By so doing fine stability will arise, and you may even identify pristine awareness....

If you become muddled and unmindful, you have slipped into laxity, or dimness. So clear up this problem, arouse your awareness, and shift your gaze. If you become distracted and excited, it is important that you lower your gaze and release your awareness. If samadhi arises in which there is nothing of which you can say, "This is meditation," and "This is conceptualization," you are slipping into a stupor, so meditate with alternating concentration and release, and recognize who is meditating. In so doing, recognize the flaws of shamatha, and eliminate them right away.[75]

REFLECTIONS ON THE PRACTICE

In the above instructions, Padmasambhava challenges you to examine the nature of your own identity as an observer and as an agent who makes choices and acts on them. While he presents this as a means for achieving shamatha, the fact that you are posing questions and investigating the nature of your experience suggests that this also may be deemed a vipashyana, or insight, practice.

Modern cognitive scientists are also challenging our everyday assumptions about the nature of the self and volition, and most of them have come to the conclusion that the source of volition is in the brain. Buddhists concur that the brain influences volition, but neurobiology has yet to present any compelling evidence that the brain is the source of volition, especially if that implies that the brain is solely responsible for the generation of volition. Neuroscientists study only physical causes of mental processes, so of course are in no position to identify any other kind of causes. That doesn't mean that nonphysical causes don't, or can't, exist. Buddhists study the mind primarily from an introspective perspective, and identify many causes of volition, and it's not at all evident that they are all physical.

The hypothesis that volitions all work through the brain, without violating any physical laws, is perfectly compatible with Buddhism, but that doesn't mean that one must accept the so-called closure principle, which states that there can be no causal influences in the physical world that are not themselves physical. The most feasible crack in the closure principle has to do with the energy-time Heisenberg Uncertainty Principle, according to which nonphysical influences may creep in for very brief moments, without violating the Principle of the Conservation of Mass-Energy, and those moments may lead to measurable effects in the macro-world.[76] This doesn't prove that there are nonphysical influences on the physical world (how could physicists ever detect them if they existed, since they have instruments to measure only physical phenomena?), but it does indicate that such influences would not violate any of the laws of physics.

In his book *The Illusion of Conscious Will* neuroscientist Daniel M. Wegner reports on research on brain mechanisms correlated with volition, with the starting assumption that physical processes in the brain alone generate all mental processes. It should come as no surprise when he finally draws his conclusion: "[I]t seems to each of us that we have conscious will. It seems we have selves. It seems we have minds. It seems we are agents. It seems we cause what we do…. [I]t is sobering and ultimately accurate to call all this an illusion."[77]

Wegner's claim to make any "ultimately accurate" statement about mind-body interactions seems especially overambitious in light of the lack of current scientific knowledge about how the neural events influence mental events and vice versa. Moreover, the immediate implication of his assertion, to which he throws the entire weight of scientific authority, is that no one is morally responsible for his or her actions. If this is an unavoidable conclusion based on unequivocally accepted scientific facts, then we must soberly apply this to our legal code and our overall appraisal of human conduct. But Wegner has leapt to his conclusion from the platform of a mass of materialistic preconceptions that were commonly assumed by psychologists and brain scientists more than a century ago. He has simply found some limited empirical evidence to support a preexisting assumption.

As an analogy, consider a researcher who measured only the vibrations created by the musical instruments as an orchestra played Beethoven's Pastoral Symphony. He would find that before anyone heard any music, the instruments vibrated in specific ways, so he might very well conclude that those vibrations are the sole cause of the symphony. What he will have left out is the role of the composer, the conductor, the skills and emotional states of the musicians, the audience, and so on. While he's right that the vibrations of the instruments played a critical role in producing the music, his eliminative approach has blinded him to a myriad of other influences, and he will be oblivious of the fact that many people can compose and play tunes in their minds, with no vibrating musical instruments exerting any causal role.

Buddhist contemplatives have drawn the conclusion that while the brain *conditions* the mind and is necessary for specific mental processes to arise as long as the substrate consciousness is embodied, the human psyche *emerges* from this underlying stream of consciousness that is embodied in life after life. This theory is compatible with all current scientific knowledge of the mind and brain, so there is nothing illogical about it, nor is it simply a faith-based proposition as far as advanced Buddhist contemplatives are concerned. Something that is purely a matter of religious faith or philosophical speculation as far as scientists are concerned may be an experientially confirmed hypothesis for Buddhist contemplatives. The demarcation between science and metaphysics is determined by the limits of experiential inquiry, not Nature or God.

The cultivation of shamatha is widely known as a means of ascertaining the relative nature of the mind, also known as the substrate consciousness, discussed in the previous chapter. But in some cases, as Padmasambhava commented, the practice of shamatha without a sign may be sufficient for ascertaining the nature of pristine awareness. This practice is one of profound inactivity. You are *being* aware of being aware, but you are not really *doing* anything. The illusory, independent ego is temporarily put out of work, and for exceptional individuals who have "little dust on their eyes," to use an ancient metaphor, this may be sufficient for fathoming the ultimate nature of the mind and its relation to reality as a whole.

In contrast to the substrate consciousness, which can be viewed as the relative ground state of the mind, pristine awareness (Tibetan: *rigpa*, Sanskrit: *vidya*) may be characterized as the absolute ground state of consciousness. Also known as primordial consciousness (*jnana*), the realization of this ultimate dimension of consciousness is a central theme of Dzogchen practice. This state entails the lowest possible state of mental activity, with the highest possible potential and degree of freedom of consciousness. Indivisible from primordial consciousness is the absolute space of phenomena (*dharmadhatu*), which transcends the duality of external and internal space.

Out of this space—nondual from primordial consciousness—emerge all the phenomena that make up our experienced world. All appearances of external and internal space, time, matter, and consciousness emerge from the absolute space of phenomena and consist of nothing other than configurations of this space. In the limited, relative vacuum of the substrate— as in the case of deep sleep—mental events specific to one individual emerge and dissolve back into that subjective space of consciousness. But all phenomena throughout time and space emerge from and dissolve back into the absolute space of phenomena—a timeless, infinite vacuum. While the relative vacuum of the substrate can be ascertained by means of the cultivation of shamatha, this absolute vacuum is usually realized only through the cultivation of vipashyana.

The experiential realization of absolute space by primordial consciousness transcends all distinctions of subject and object, mind and matter, indeed, all words and concepts. Such insight does not entail the meeting of a subjective mode of consciousness with an objective space, but rather the nondual realization of the intrinsic *unity* of absolute space and primordial consciousness. While the absolute space of phenomena is the fundamental nature of the experienced world, primordial consciousness is the fundamental nature of the mind. All such distinctions between subject and object, mind and matter, are regarded as mere conceptual fabrications.

The unity of absolute space and primordial consciousness is the Great Perfection, often referred to as the "one taste" of all phenomena. The substrate consciousness may be called a relative, or false, vacuum state of consciousness, for it is different from the substrate that it ascertains; it is qualified by distinct experiences of bliss, luminosity, and nonconceptuality; it is ascertained when the mind is withdrawn from the external world; and it is bound by time and causality—specific to a given individual. Therefore, despite its vacuity, it has an internal structure. The unity of absolute space and primordial consciousness, on the other hand, is the absolute, or true, vacuum. Although it, too, is imbued with the qualities of bliss, luminosity, and nonconceptuality, these are not present as distinct attributes (as they are in the substrate consciousness).

When one realizes the substrate consciousness by achieving shamatha, mental afflictions are only temporarily suppressed, but as a result of realizing primordial consciousness, it is said that all mental afflictions (*klesha*) and obscurations (*avarana*) are eliminated forever. Likewise, the bliss that is experienced when resting in the relative ground state of consciousness is limited and transient, whereas the inconceivable bliss that is innate to the absolute ground state of primordial consciousness is limitless and eternal. By ascertaining the substrate consciousness, you realize the relative nature of individual consciousness, but in the realization of primordial consciousness, the scope of awareness becomes boundless. Likewise, the creative potential of consciousness that is accessed through shamatha is limited, whereas that which is unveiled through ultimate contemplative insight allegedly knows no bounds. Thus, in reference to the absolute ground state of consciousness, the Buddha declared, "All phenomena are preceded by the mind. When the mind is comprehended, all phenomena are comprehended. By bringing the mind under control, all things are brought under control."[78]

INTERLUDE DREAM YOGA—DAYTIME PRACTICE

By closely attending to everything that arises with discerning mindfulness, you will gain a clearer and clearer awareness of the nature of waking reality, and that, in turn, can lead to lucidity in your dreams. In the daytime practice in preparation for lucid dreaming, you specifically took note of dreamsigns, and you conducted state checks to determine whether you were awake or dreaming. In the Buddhist view, all of us who are not yet buddhas, or awakened ones, are leading our lives in a dreamlike state. So the daytime practice presented in this interlude is to help us realize the illusory nature of waking reality.

According to classical Buddhist philosophy—a form of empirical pluralism—real phenomena are those that can causally influence other phenomena and be influenced by them, whereas unreal phenomena are those that are merely conceptually projected on the world of perceptual experience.[79] There are three classes of real phenomena: (1) material phenomena, which are composed of elementary particles, (2) cognitive phenomena, which consciously apprehend objects, and (3) abstract composites, such as time, justice, institutions, and people. Unreal phenomena do exist, but only by conventional agreement, and they have no causal efficacy of their own. They include such things as borders between countries, ownership, and titles. These are conceptual designations that communities of people agree on, so they exist *for them*, but they have no existence apart from those conventional agreements.

In addition to such valid conventions, we also conceptually project things that have no basis in reality at all. In the classical Buddhist worldview, we are prone to imagine things as being more static and durable than they really are. In these ways we mistake the impermanent for the permanent. We also regard things, such as wealth, fame, and sensory pleasures, as sources of happiness, whereas in reality they are not. In these ways we mistake things that are not truly satisfying as being so. Thirdly, we commonly look upon things as "I" or "mine" that are in fact simply phenomena, arising in dependence upon impersonal causes and conditions. In these ways we mistake things that are not an immutable, unitary, independent self as being such a self or belonging to it.

By mindfully and discerningly attending to all kinds of perceptual appearances—material, mental, and otherwise—we can begin to distinguish between what appears to be our immediate sensory experience and our conceptual projections. In doing so, we start to discover the extent to which our waking experience is illusory. But the dreamlike nature of our experienced world may go a lot deeper than that. In the *Perfection of Wisdom Sutras* the Buddha makes the more radical claim that the world of our waking experience is fundamentally no more real than a dream. In a nonlucid dream, we mistakenly grasp onto all objective and subjective appearances as if they were inherently real, bearing their own intrinsic existence. Likewise, in the normal (nonlucid) waking state we do the same thing, imagining the physical world to be really "out there," existing independently of our conceptual constructs; and we grasp onto our thoughts and other subjective experiences as being really "in here," existing by their own inherent nature. In philosophical terms, we *reify*—or project as a substantial, independent existence—everything we experience while awake and asleep.

All schools of Buddhist philosophy recognize the problem of seeking to fathom a world that purportedly exists independently of the mind that is seeking to understand it.[80] In the "Middle Way," or Madhyamaka, philosophy—which is to classical Buddhist philosophy what Einstein's theory of relativity is to classical physics—reality can be understood only in relation to specific cognitive frames of reference.[81] Subject and object are always interrelated, and neither can exist without the other, implying a kind of universal, ontological relativity. Much as Einstein refuted the notion of absolute space, Madhyamikas, or advocates of the Middle Way, refute the existence of an absolutely objective physical world as well as absolutely subjective minds. Our very notions of subject and object and of mind and matter are conceptual constructs created by human minds, and they have no meaning independent of our conceptual frameworks.

From the Madhyamaka perspective, all known objects exist relative to the perceptual and conceptual frames of reference by which they are known. The perceived color red does not exist independently of the visual awareness of it, and no entities postulated by mathematics and science— from non-Euclidean geometry to superstrings to galactic clusters—exist independently of the minds that have conceived them. Phenomena are literally brought into existence in dependence upon our conceptual designations of them.

Phenomena *appear* to exist inherently, independently of our conceptual frameworks, and we deludedly grasp onto them as *existing* just as they appear. But this simply perpetuates the dreamlike nature of experience of all kinds. When you become lucid in a dream, you begin to recognize that things are not as they appear, and now your challenge is to recognize the extent to which things in the waking state are no more real than a dream.

THE PRACTICE OF DAYTIME DREAM YOGA

The daytime practice of dream yoga can be approached first from the perspective of classical Buddhist philosophy and then in terms of the relativistic Middle Way. Through the close application of mindfulness, take as your "dreamsigns" anything that appears to be permanent, ultimately satisfying, and as belonging to an independent self. Wake up to the fact that you are conflating your conceptual projections with the immediate contents of experience, and recall the Buddha's statement, "In the seen there is only the seen; in the heard, there is only the heard; in the sensed, there is only the sensed; in the mentally perceived, there is only the mentally perceived."

As you incorporate the Middle Way view into your daytime practice, you may follow the instructions of Padmasambhava:

It is like this: all phenomena do not [inherently] existent, but they appear to exist and are established as various things, like white and red. That which is impermanent is grasped as permanent, and that which is not truly existent is grasped as being truly existent. Although it is said that this cause of the bondage of all beings is like an illusion, due to grasping onto the true existence of deceptive appearances, phenomena now appear as truly existent. These originally arose from insubstantiality, they now appear even though they are not [inherently] existent, and in the end they will become nothing. Consider that since these things, which are without permanence, stability, or immutability, have no inherent nature, they are like illusions.[82]

Whenever you experience anything as existing independently of your conceptual framework, recognize its dreamlike nature, and in this way you can begin to become lucid during the waking state.

STAGE 9: ATTENTIONAL BALANCE ● ● ●

With only the slightest exertion of effort, you proceed from the eighth attentional stage to the ninth, known as _attentional balance._ You are now able to maintain flawless samadhi, effortlessly and continuously for at least four hours. Due to the power of deep familiarization with this training, you can slip into meditative equipoise, free of even the subtlest traces of laxity and excitation, with no effort at all. This is not to say that your attention is irreversibly balanced. If for some reason you discontinue the practice, you will find that laxity and excitation erode your attentional equipoise. They have not been irreversibly eliminated. But if you maintain a contemplative lifestyle and keep your attention honed through regular practice, this wonderful degree of sanity can be yours for life.

To reach this point will almost certainly require many months, or even a few years, of continuous, full-time practice. You'll never succeed if you work at this even very intensively for only brief intervals, taking many breaks in between. Likewise, the higher stages of shamatha practice will not be achieved by engaging in many brief retreats of weeks or a few months at a time. It requires long, continuous practice without interruption. There are no shortcuts.

Contemplatives who have achieved this ninth stage of attentional balance describe the quality of this experience simply as "perfection." The mind has come to a yet deeper state of stillness and serenity, likened now to Mount Meru, the king of mountains. It would be understandable to conclude that you have now fully achieved shamatha. You are almost there.

THE PRACTICE: AWARENESS WITHOUT AN OBJECT

Here are quintessential instructions by Padmasambhava on the practice of shamatha with no object apart from awareness itself:

> Vacantly direct your eyes into the space in front of you. See that thoughts pertaining to the past, future, and present, as well as wholesome, unwholesome, and ethically neutral thoughts, together with all the causes, assembly, and dispersal of thoughts of the three times are completely cut off. Bring no concepts to mind. Let the mind, like a cloudless sky, be clear, empty, and evenly devoid of grasping; and settle it in utter vacuity. By doing so there arises the quiescence of joy, luminosity, and nonconceptuality. Examine whether or not there enters into that attachment, hatred, clinging, grasping, laxity, or excitation, and recognize the difference between virtues and vices.

REFLECTIONS ON THE PRACTICE

√ While all the schools of Tibetan Buddhism adhere to the same basic philosophical perspective, the understanding of primordial consciousness is an enduring area of debate. The difference lies in whether you see the enlightened consciousness as something to be cultivated or something that is merely uncovered. This debate has practical implications for attention meditation.

The Dzogchen and Mahamudra traditions, most strongly associated with the Nyingma and Kagyü orders of Tibetan Buddhism, respectively, view the pristine awareness as a perfectly enlightened state of consciousness that is already present, but obscured by mental afflictions and other obscurations. Since all the qualities of primordial consciousness, or buddha-nature, are believed to be implicit in ordinary human consciousness, the exceptional degrees of attentional stability are also considered innate to the nature of awareness itself. Ultimately, those qualities don't need to be developed; they are waiting to be discovered, and the above practice is precisely designed to do just that.

The Geluk and Sakya orders of Tibetan Buddhism generally regard the buddha-nature as our *potential* for achieving enlightenment, but the mind must be developed in various ways in order to achieve the immeasurable qualities of wisdom, compassion, and creativity of a buddha. Likewise, the Geluk and Sakya orders most commonly emphasize shamatha techniques aimed at developing stability and vividness by focusing the mind on "signs," or meditation objects.

Nevertheless, just as Nyingma and Kagyü lamas frequently teach a variety of shamatha techniques using signs, so do Geluk and Sakya lamas acknowledge the value of practicing shamatha by resting awareness in its own nature. Thus the distinctions should not be conceived too rigidly. Tsongkhapa, the fifteenth-century founder of the Geluk order, describes this practice as follows:

> In the cultivation of simple nonconceptual attention, without focusing on any object, such as a deity, resolve, "I will settle the mind without thinking about any object." Then, without letting the attention become scattered, avoid distraction.[83]

The First Panchen Lama, also part of the Geluk order, describes this practice in this way:

> Be unrelenting toward ideation, and each time you observe the nature of any ideation that arises, those thoughts will vanish by themselves, following which, a vacuity appears. Likewise, if you examine the mind also when it remains without fluctuation, you will see an unobscured, clear, and vivid vacuity, without any difference between the former and latter states. Among meditators that is acclaimed and called "the fusion of stillness and dispersion."[84]

Finally, the late Sakya master Deshung Rinpoche, in his discussion of the question "Is it 'natural' not to be natural?" explains this technique in this way:

> Meditate as follows: sit in the correct meditation posture and be as natural as possible. Remain in the present, focusing on neither the past nor future. Sitting like this, you will see that it is "natural" not to be natural. Thoughts arise. The point is not to be victimized by these thoughts—simply let them pass and rest in the clear aspect of mind. In this way, you will eventually obtain insight; subsequently, you will develop this insight in a stable fashion and will maintain it even when engaged in other activities. At that point, the sense of the emptiness of phenomena will always be with you.[85]

In the above description of the practice of dwelling in the clear aspect of mind, Deshung Rinpoche claims that this practice may lead to a realization of emptiness, the ultimate nature of phenomena. And in his explanation of the practice of shamatha without a sign, Padmasambhava comments that by meditating in this way, one may even identify pristine awareness. It needs to be emphasized, though, that only in rare cases does shamatha practice of any kind directly yield insight into emptiness or pristine awareness. The purpose of shamatha meditation is to develop or unveil the stability and vividness of attention. This is like developing a telescope for the precise, penetrating observation of mental phenomena, including the nature of consciousness itself. In this way, shamatha can be viewed as "contemplative technology," whereas the practice of vipashyana is a kind of "contemplative science." The sequence between shamatha and vipashyana makes perfect sense: first refine your powers of attention, then use them to explore and purify the mind, which can be directly examined only through first-person observation.

The Buddha emphasizes this sequence countless times, as when he poses the question, "What, monks, is the sufficing condition of knowledge and vision of things as they really are?" and responds, "It should be answered, 'Concentration' (samadhi)."[86] Kamalashila echoed this same theme when he wrote, "Because the mind moves like a river, it does not remain stationary without the foundation of quiescence. The mind that is not established in equipoise is incapable of knowing reality. The Buddha too, declared, 'The mind that is established in equipoise comes to know reality as it is."[87] And Shantideva spoke for the entire Mahayana tradition when he declared, "Realizing that one who is well endowed with insight by way of shamatha eradicates mental afflictions, one should first seek shamatha."[88]

Many students of Tibetan Buddhism are taught devotional preliminary practices (ngöndro) to tantric meditation and encouraged to focus on these until they complete them. This raises the question of whether it is best to achieve shamatha first and then apply oneself to these preliminary practices, or vice versa. The advantage of accomplishing shamatha first is that you can then apply your refined attention to the preliminaries, enormously enhancing the efficacy of those practices. On the other hand, if you complete your preliminaries first, this will purify your mind so that you encounter fewer obstacles in your practice of shamatha. The late Kalu Rinpoche, an eminent meditation master in the Kagyü tradition, responded that the achievement of shamatha is essential, but either of the above two sequences may be followed, depending on your own personal inclination.[89]

Given the widespread consensus concerning the vital role of shamatha in Buddhist contemplative practice, one might expect that it would be widely practiced and that many people would accomplish it. Oddly enough, there has long been a strong tendency among Tibetan Buddhist contemplatives to marginalize shamatha in favor of more advanced practices. Tsongkhapa commented on this oversight in the fifteenth century when he said, "There seem to be very few who achieve even shamatha,"[90] and Düdjom Lingpa commented four centuries later, "Among unrefined people in this degenerate era, very few appear to achieve more than fleeting stability."[91]

During numerous conversations with seasoned recluses and with His Holiness the Dalai Lama, I have tried to discover whether this statement holds true nowadays. The consensus is that the actual achievement of shamatha today among Tibetan Buddhist contemplatives, both in Tibet and living in exile, is not unknown, but it is exceptionally rare.

The Sri Lankan Theravada scholar and contemplative Balangoda Anandamaitreya told me that despite the fact that there were hundreds of Buddhist meditators in numerous hermitages throughout his country, only a small handful had achieved genuine shamatha. Most focused almost entirely on vipashyana, sometimes to the exclusion of shamatha altogether.

Shamatha practice predates the Buddha, and some Buddhists dismiss it on the grounds that shamatha practice by itself does not liberate the mind. Some Mahayana Buddhists marginalize it on the grounds that it is common to Theravada Buddhism, which they regard as an "inferior vehicle" of spiritual practice. And there are Tibetan Buddhists who similarly overlook it in favor of more esoteric tantric practices. In all cases, such people disregard the teachings of the Buddha as well as the most authoritative contemplatives in their own traditions.

The achievement of shamatha does not mean that you have realized emptiness, the bedrock insight necessary for Buddhist liberation. And the realization of emptiness does not mean that you have recognized pristine awareness. You may indeed gain some insight into emptiness without having achieved shamatha, but that realization will not be durable or capable of fully purifying your mind of its afflictive tendencies. Likewise, you may receive "pointing-out instructions" that arouse in you an experience of pristine awareness, but if you have not deeply cultivated the stability and vividness of your attention, it is unlikely that you will be able to sustain that experience.

INTERLUDE DREAM YOGA—NIGHTTIME PRACTICE

When contemplatives who are adept at dream yoga enter into a lucid dream, they can have the satisfaction of knowing that everything in their experience consists of just the kinds of phenomena they wish to study: they all consist of consciousness. A lucid dream is a perfect laboratory for the first-person study of the mind. To ensure that their research will go well, various factors need to be taken into account: (1) they must maintain an ethical way of life that supports the cultivation of mental balance and contemplative insight; (2) they must develop enhanced degrees of mental balance, especially shamatha, so that they are properly equipped to experientially probe the nature of consciousness; and (3) they must know how to rigorously investigate the mind using the methods of vipashyana and other modes of contemplative inquiry.

The first step in the nighttime practice of dream yoga is to recognize the dream and maintain the stability and vividness of that recognition. The second step is to practice transforming the contents of the dream, both in terms of your own presence in the dream and in terms of everything that "objectively" appears to you. Even though you are lucid, recognizing the dream-state for what it is, phenomena in the dream still appear as if they existed "from their own side," independently of your experience and conceptual framework.

When you look at a wall, for example, you will see it as being something firm and hard, and if you reach out to touch it, this perception will be confirmed. But the dreamed wall does not consist of any configurations of mass-energy. It has no atomic density, nor does your dreamed body, so there should be no reason why you can't walk right through the wall. Nevertheless, most lucid dreamers have a hard time, at least at their first attempts, walking through walls. Even though they "know" the wall has no objective existence apart from their experience of it, they still can't walk through it. Some have ingeniously found that they can walk through it backward. Another reported that when he first tried this, he made it halfway through the wall, then got stuck, as if it were a gelatinous substance. Many lucid dreamers find it relatively easy to fly, but walking on water and moving through solid objects may be more challenging. In this phase of dream yoga, you keep working at transforming all kinds of dream phenomena, exploring whether there is anything that is objectively resistant to the powers of your imagination. In this way, you begin to fathom the nature of dreaming consciousness and its creative powers.

When you engage in such practice for a prolonged period, this may catalyze the occurrence of nightmares, and in the third stage of dream yoga, when you encounter horrific things and situations, your task is not to transform them but rather to surrender to them with the full awareness that nothing in the dream can harm you. This is analogous to the earlier practice of settling the mind in its natural state, when you recognized that nothing can harm your mind, whether or not thoughts have ceased. Your own presence in the dream and everything else consist of illusory manifestations of consciousness, and as long as you don't reify them—take them to be more real and substantial than they actually are—nothing can hurt you.

In a further stage of dream yoga you release the dream, letting it vanish back into the space of the mind, and rest in a silent, luminous awareness of awareness itself, devoid of any other content. This is the state of lucid dreamless sleep, and in this state you may apprehend the substrate consciousness, and possibly even pristine awareness. For this, the daytime practice of shamatha without a sign is an excellent preparation.

The Tibetan Buddhist tradition views the processes of (1) falling asleep, (2) dreaming, and (3) waking as parallel to the processes of (1) dying, (2) passing through the intermediate state (*bardo*) after death and prior to one's next birth, and (3) taking rebirth. In this way, each day-and-night cycle is a microcosm of the entire cycle of death and rebirth. For this reason, the primary reason Tibetan Buddhists practice dream yoga is to prepare them for the intermediate state, which is said to have a dreamlike quality. If you do not recognize the intermediate state for what it is, you will respond to events in that transitional period simply out of habit, as in a nonlucid dream. But if you recognize the intermediate state and maintain a clear awareness of the nature of this phase of existence, you open up whole dimensions of freedom, as in a lucid dream. In this way you can follow the path of spiritual awakening in all states of consciousness—during the daytime, while meditating, in dreamless sleep, and while dreaming. You have transformed your entire existence into spiritual practice.

THE PRACTICE OF NIGHTTIME DREAM YOGA

For instructions on the nighttime practice of dream yoga we return once again to the teachings of Padmasambhava:

> Lie in the sleeping-lion position, and bring forth a powerful yearning to recognize the dream-state as the dream-state; and while doing so, fall asleep without being interrupted by any other thoughts. Even if you do not apprehend it at the first try, repeat this many times, and earnestly do it with powerful yearning. In the morning when you wake up, forcefully and distinctly consider, "Not a single one of any of the dreams I had last night remains when I wake up. Likewise, not a single one of all these daytime appearances today will appear tonight in my dreams. There is no difference between the dreams of the day and the night, so they are illusions, they are dreams...."

> At first, there will be more dreams, then they will become clearer, and then they will be apprehended. In the event of a frightening circumstance, it is easy to recognize, "This is a dream." It is difficult for it to be apprehended spontaneously, but if it is so apprehended, this is stable....

While apprehending the dream-state, consider, "Since this is now a dream-body, it can be transformed in any way." Whatever arises in the dream, be it demonic apparitions, monkeys, people, dogs, and so on…practice multiplying them by emanation and changing them into anything you like….

Seeing through the dream: Apprehend the dream-state and go to the bank of a great river. Consider, "Since I am a mental-body of a dream, there is nothing for the river to carry away." By jumping into the river, you will be carried away by a current of bliss and emptiness. At first, because of the clinging of self-grasping, you won't dare, but that won't happen once you have grown accustomed to it. Similarly by seeing through all such things as fire, precipices, and carnivorous animals, all fears will arise as samadhi….

Lie down in the sleeping-lion posture, with your head pointing north. Slightly hold your breath, curve your neck, and steadily cast your gaze upwards. Focus your attention clearly and vividly on a visualized orb of white light at your heart. With clear, vivid awareness in the nature of light, fall asleep. In the dream-state the clear light of awareness will appear like the essence of limpid space, clear and empty, free of the intellect.[92]

In the "sleeping-lion posture," you lie on your right side, with your right hand beneath your right cheek and your left hand resting on your left thigh. This is the position in which the Buddha reportedly passed away, and it has been strongly recommended ever since as a suitable posture in which to sleep mindfully.

According to Tibetan Buddhism, appearances in a dream arise from the substrate consciousness and vanish back into it. Since they are entirely formations of your own consciousness, without any constraints from sensory inputs from the physical world, they can be transformed at will, but only if you fully recognize that you are dreaming. Most of us assume that we are lucid—clearly aware of the nature of our existence—while in the waking state, but in comparison to a buddha, we are sleepwalkers, moving through life and death in a nonlucid dream. According to the Dzogchen view, everything in the entire universe consists of phenomena arising from the primordial unity of pristine awareness and the absolute space of phenomena. If we viewed reality from that perspective, instead of from the limited vantage point of a human psyche, the whole world would appear as a dream, and we would be the dreamer. The potentials of freedom for those who are truly awakened are infinite.

STAGE 10: SHAMATHA ● ● ●

F ollowing the realization of the ninth stage of attentional balance, after months or years of continuous, full-time practice, you are primed to achieve shamatha. The nine preceding stages entail many incremental changes, but the actual accomplishment of shamatha involves a radical transition in your body and mind. You will be like a butterfly emerging from its cocoon. This shift is characterized by specific experiences that take place within a discrete, relatively brief period of time.

According to accounts from the Indo-Tibetan tradition of Buddhism, the first sign of the achievement of shamatha is the experience of a sense of heaviness and numbness on the top of the head. This allegedly happens to anyone who experiences this transition, regardless of the specific method followed. It is said to feel as if a palm were being placed on the top of your shaved head. It's not unpleasant or harmful, just unusual.

Something remarkable must be taking place in the cortical region of your brain at this point, but so far, no one has monitored the brain correlates of this shift using magnetic resonance imaging or an electroencephalograph. This physical sensation on the top of the head is symptomatic of a shift in your nervous system (or network of vital energies) that is correlated with gaining freedom from mental *dysfunction (daushtulya)*, a general state of mental imbalance characterized by stiffness, rigidity, and unwieldiness. Consequently, you achieve a state of mental *pliancy (prashrabdhi)*, in which your mind is fit and supple like never before.

From a contemplative perspective, when the mind is dysfunctional, or prone to laxity and excitation, it is hard to generate enthusiasm for healing the afflictions of your mind or for devoting yourself to virtuous mental activity. Once you are free of such mental dysfunction, you can focus your mind without resistance on any meaningful object or task, and such a mind is now said to be fit, or serviceable. This is the key to achieving optimal mental performance.

Following this sense of pressure on the top of your head, you experience the movement of vital energies moving in your body, and when they have coursed everywhere throughout your body, you feel as if you were filled with the power of this dynamic energy. You are now freed of physical dysfunction, so your body feels buoyant and light like never before. Both your body and mind are now imbued with an exceptional degree of pliancy, which makes them remarkably fit for engaging in all kinds of mental training and other meaningful activities.

When physical pliancy initially arises, the vital energies catalyze an extraordinary sense of physical bliss, which then triggers an equally exceptional experience of mental bliss. This rush of physical and mental rapture is transient, which is a good thing, for it so captivates the attention that you can do little else except enjoy it. Gradually it subsides and you are freed from the turbulence caused by this intense joy. Your attention settles down in perfect stability and vividness. You have now achieved shamatha.

Padmasambhava described this state as follows:

> Flawless shamatha is like an oil-lamp that is unmoved by the air. Wherever the awareness is placed, it is unwaveringly present; awareness is vividly clear, without being sullied by laxity, lethargy, or dimness; wherever the awareness is directed, it is steady and sharply pointed; and unmoved by adventitious thoughts, it is straight. Thus, a flawless meditative state arises in your mindstream; and until this happens, it is important that you settle the mind in its natural state. Without genuine shamatha arising in your mindstream, even if awareness is pointed out, it becomes nothing more than an object of intellectual understanding. So you are left simply giving lip-service to the view, and there is the danger that you may succumb to dogmatism.

Thus, the root of all meditative states depends upon this, so do not be introduced to pristine awareness too soon, but practice until you have a fine experience of stability.[93]

The Theravada tradition gives this specific description of achieving shamatha by way of mindfulness of the respiration: You begin this practice, as described earlier, by focusing on the tactile sensations of the breath, which are the "sign" for preliminary practice (*parikamma-nimitta*). Eventually you shift your attention to the acquired sign (*uggaha-nimitta*) of the breath, which becomes your meditative object until you achieve shamatha, at which point a third sign appears spontaneously. This is called the counterpart sign (*patibhaga-nimitta*) of the breath, which is a subtle, emblematic representation of the whole quality of the air element.[94] Buddhaghosa described this sign as follows:

> The counterpart sign appears as if breaking out from the acquired sign, and a hundred times a thousand times more purified, like a looking-glass disk drawn from its case, like a mother-of-pearl dish well washed, like the moon's disk coming out from behind a cloud, like cranes against a thunder cloud. But it has neither color nor shape...it is born only in the perception in one who has obtained concentration, being a mere model of appearance.[95]

In Buddhism, all ordinary states of human consciousness, while awake or asleep, are said to belong to the *desire realm,* which is so called because this dimension of consciousness is dominated by sensual desires. All the nine stages leading up to the achievement of shamatha also belong to this realm, and it is only with the achievement of the mental and physical pliancy of shamatha that you gain access to the *form realm.* This is a subtle dimension of consciousness that transcends the realm of the physical senses, similar in some respects to the world of pure ideas envisioned by Plato, or the archetypal world hypothesized by Jung. Upon gaining access to the form realm, your consciousness continues to be structured by very subtle concepts that stem from a deeper source than the human psyche. Theravada Buddhists discuss a variety of counterpart signs that are perceived once you gain access to the form realm. These signs appear to include rarefied, archetypal representations of phenomena experienced in the desire realm, including the elements of solidity, fluidity, heat, motility, the four colors of blue, yellow, red, and white, and light and space.

The initial achievement of shamatha is described as *preliminary* or as *access* to the full realization of the first meditative stabilization (*dhyana*). The Buddha declared that with the achievement of the first meditative stabilization, one is for the first time temporarily freed from five types of obstructions (*avarana*), or hindrances (*nivarana*), that disrupt the balance of the mind.[96] These are (1) sensual craving, (2) malice, (3) lethargy and drowsiness, (4) excitation and anxiety, and (5) uncertainty. Buddhaghosa commented that as soon as the counterpart sign arises, the hindrances are quite suppressed, the defilements subside, and the mind becomes concentrated in access concentration.[97]

When you first gain the mental and physical pliancy associated with the freedom from these hindrances, you experience a rush of bliss that appears to be a symptom of achieving an unprecedented level of mental health. The Buddha was presumably referring to this bliss as a sufficing condition, or immediate catalyst, for the achievement of samadhi.[98] Here is one of his more detailed accounts of this experience:[99]

> Separated from pleasures of sense, separated from unwholesome states of mind, one attains to and abides in the first stabilization, which is accompanied by coarse examination and precise investigation, born of seclusion, and is joyful and blissful. And one drenches, fills, completely fills and pervades one's body with joy and bliss, born of seclusion so that there is nowhere in one's body that is not pervaded by it.

With the realization of access to the first stabilization, five mental factors associated with that level of samadhi arise, which directly counteract the five hindrances:

1. The factor of *coarse examination*, which counters the combined hinderances of *lethargy and drowsiness*
2. The factor of *precise investigation*, which counters the hindrance of *uncertainty*
3. The factor of *well-being*, which counters the hindrance of *malice*
4. The factor of *bliss*, which counters the combined hindrances of *excitation and anxiety*
5. The factor of *single-pointed attention*, which counters *sensual craving*

The beauty of this is that those very healing factors that can counter the obstacles to achieving mental balance emerge naturally through the process of stabilizing the mind. The practice of shamatha reveals the profound capacity of the mind to heal itself.

A significant difference between access to the first stabilization and the actual state of that stabilization is that in the former, you gain only a tenuous freedom from the five hindrances, whereas in the latter, your immunity to them is stronger. There is a similar difference in the stability of the five factors of stabilization. There is a corresponding difference in the length of time you can remain immersed in such sublime states of focused attention. With access to the first stabilization, you can effortlessly remain in samadhi for at least four hours at a stretch, without the slightest perturbation from either subtle laxity or excitation. But once you have achieved the actual state of the first stabilization, samadhi can be sustained, according to Buddhaghosa, "for a whole night and a whole day, just as a healthy man, after rising from his seat, could stand a whole day."[100]

Due to deep attentional stability, you may feel as if your sleep is suffused with samadhi and many pure dreams. Your sense of attentional vividness becomes so great that you feel that you could count the atoms of the pillars and walls of your house, and your attention is highly focused throughout all your daily activities. These exceptional degrees of stability and vividness of your awareness carry over, to a considerably degree, in your consciousness after you arise from your meditation practice and engage in your daily affairs, when your mind returns to the desire realm. When your mind disengages from activity, it naturally slips back into a space-like state of awareness, and physical and mental pliancy arise very swiftly.

The most important effect of shamatha that lingers on between meditation sessions is a temporary, relative freedom from afflictive thoughts and emotions. It's not that they don't arise at all anymore, but they occur less frequently, with less intensity, and for shorter periods. In particular, you are mostly free of the five hindrances—as long as you don't lose your attentional balance. Between meditation sessions, you retain an exceptional degree of both kinds of pliancy and fitness, which causes you to be naturally inclined to acting virtuously. Shamatha adepts report that due to bodily fitness, you have no feelings of physical heaviness or discomfort, your spine becomes "straight like a golden pillar," and your body feels blissful, as if it were bathed with warm milk. Due to mental fitness, you are now fully in control of the mind, virtually free of sadness and grief and continuously experiencing a state of well-being. As the Buddha declared, those who have achieved any state of meditative stabilization abide in happiness here and now.[101]

THE PRACTICE: RESTING IN LUMINOUS VACUITY

As described earlier, the achievement of shamatha by way of mindfulness of breathing is marked by the first appearance of the counterpart sign of the air element. But because the five factors of stabilization (coarse examination, precise investigation, well-being, bliss, and single-pointed attention) are not strong in access concentration, you will find it very difficult to sustain your attention on this very subtle mental image. Your mind will slip into the _bhavanga,_ or the ground of becoming, which is a relative vacuum state of consciousness, voided of all thoughts, mental imagery, and sense perceptions. Buddhaghosa likens this to a young child who is lifted up and stood on its feet, but repeatedly falls down on the ground.[102] If you wish to proceed beyond access concentration to the actual state of the first stabilization, you steadfastly focus on the counterpart sign until you can maintain your attention on it for a whole day and night. But if you are content with this level of access concentration and wish to use it as a basis for your practice of vipashyana, or contemplative insight, then you release the counterpart sign and rest for a time in the ground of becoming.

It is common for contemplatives to settle for access concentration. Asanga advised that as soon as this state of shamatha is achieved, the entire continuum and flow of one's attention should be single-pointedly focused inward on the mind. In this practice, divest your consciousness of all signs and thoughts, and allow it to remain in a state of tranquillity. If you have achieved shamatha by focusing on a mental image, you should now release that image and rest in a state of consciousness free of appearances. At this point, with the entirety of your awareness withdrawn from your physical senses, and with consciousness disengaged from all discursive thought and imagery, you experience a nondual awareness of consciousness itself. In that way, the relative nature of consciousness is directly perceived, and yet it is ungraspable and undemonstrable.

Once you have achieved shamatha, you can enter it at will. While abiding in this state, the whole of your attention is focused single-pointedly, withdrawn from the physical senses, discursive thoughts, and mental imagery, and is immersed in the substrate consciousness. In this state, no "signs" appear to the mind, or if they do on rare occasions due to a temporary lapse of mindfulness, they quickly disappear by themselves, as your mind rests in the luminous vacuity of the substrate consciousness. No appearances of your own body or anything else arise, so you feel as if the mind has become indivisible with space. Your mind has become so still and divorced from discursive thoughts that you feel you could remain in meditation uninterruptedly for months or even years, with no awareness of the passage of time. While your mind is immersed in this state, it is suffused with an inner sense of well-being, in which it is impossible for unwholesome thoughts or any kind of discomfort to arise. Düdjom Lingpa describes this experience as follows:

> Eventually all coarse and subtle thoughts will be calmed in the empty expanse of the essential nature of your mind. You will become still in an unfluctuating state, in which you will experience joy like the warmth of a fire, clarity like the dawn, and nonconceptuality like an ocean unmoved by waves.[103]

While abiding in shamatha, you may have little or no experience of the passage of time, for the sense of time requires memory, which is activated through conceptualization; so in the absence of conceptualization, you dwell in a state of consciousness that feels timeless. Nevertheless, before entering meditative equipoise, you can cue yourself to emerge from meditation after a designated period, or you can prepare your mind to be aroused from samadhi by a specific sound or other sensory stimulus. When you do emerge from meditation in which your awareness was removed from all sensory experience, you feel as if your body is suddenly coming into being.

REFLECTIONS ON THE PRACTICE

How Long Does It Take?

How long does it take to achieve shamatha if one is well prepared and practices diligently and continuously in a conducive environment, with good companions and under the skillful guidance of an experienced mentor? As mentioned in the introduction, the Tibetan oral tradition states that under such optimal conditions, a person of "sharp faculties" may achieve shamatha in three months, one of "medium faculties" in six months, and a person of "dull faculties" may achieve it in nine months. This may well be true for monks and nuns who begin their shamatha practice after years of study and training in ethics. But in the modern world, this appears to be an overly optimistic forecast. Consider that five thousand hours of training, at a rate of fifty hours each week for fifty weeks of the year, is the amount of time commonly required to achieve expertise in a high-level skill. To reach an exceptionally high level of mastery, ten thousand hours may be required. If we place shamatha training in this context, it may give us some idea about the degree of commitment needed to achieve such attentional skills.

Given the many profound psychological, societal, and environmental differences between people living in industrialized nations and in traditional societies such as rural Tibet, it is impossible to predict with accuracy how long it may take people living in our modern world to achieve shamatha. But there are some encouraging signs that significant progress can be made. At the end of the one-year shamatha retreat led by Gen

Lamrimpa in 1988, one meditator sat four sessions each day, each one last-ing three hours. Another sat for just two sessions, each more than seven hours long. Neither one, according to Gen Lamrimpa, had achieved shamatha at that point, but both had made very good progress. When they arose from their meditations after so many hours, it felt to them as if no time had passed at all, and their bodies and minds were filled with blissful and relaxed sensations.

The Threefold Training

The "threefold training" of ethical discipline, concentration, and wisdom comprises the essential framework of the Buddhist path of liberation. The first training, in ethical discipline, consists of the three factors of *right speech, right action,* and *right livelihood.* The primary purpose of this first level of training is to support the cultivation of focused attention, which has the function of balancing the mind, thereby elevating it to higher, more serene, blissful, and radiant states of consciousness. Such purification is not possible without ethical discipline, in which mental imbalances are reduced through restraint from unwholesome physical, verbal, and mental behavior. As a result of training in ethical discipline, the mind is imbued with self-confidence, absence of remorse, fearlessness, and inward purity and serenity, which makes it suitable for the second training, in concen-tration. Similarly, the achievement of an exceptional degree of concen-tration and mental balance (through the cultivation of shamatha) is necessary to progress fully in the third training, in wisdom.

The training in concentration consists of *right effort, right mindfulness,* and *right concentration.* Within this training, right effort and right mindfulness fulfill an essentially supportive role, the former by exerting the mind, the latter balancing it. Together they support the achievement of right con-centration, which is defined by the Buddha in terms of the attainment of states of meditative stabilization. Such degrees of mental balance (concen-tration), the Buddha declared, are a necessary prerequisite for gaining expe-riential knowledge and vision of things as they really are (wisdom).[104] This view is shared by the entire Indian Mahayana tradition, as expressed by Shantideva: "Realizing that one who is well endowed with vipashyana by way of shamatha eradicates mental afflictions, one should first seek shamatha."[105] Tsongkhapa illustrated the relation between shamatha and vipashyana with the following metaphor:

> When examining a tapestry in a dark room, if you illuminate it with a radiant, steady lamp, you can vividly examine the images. If the lamp is dim, or, though bright, flickers in the wind, your observation will be impaired. Likewise, when analyzing the nature of any phenomenon, support penetrating intelligence with unwavering, sustained, voluntary attention, and you can clearly observe the real nature of the phenomenon under investigation.[106]

The primary reason such an exceptional degree of concentration, or samadhi, is needed is that only with the achievement of access to the first stabilization are you freed from the five hindrances. Until such freedom is achieved, the Buddha stated, "One considers himself as indebted, sick, in bonds, enslaved, and lost in a desert track,"[107] and it is not possible to know one's own "welfare, another's welfare, or the welfare of both, and realize the excellence of knowledge and vision befitting the noble ones, transcending the human state."[108] The achievement of shamatha provides the necessary foundation in mental and physical pliancy and fitness to be able to fully develop contemplative insight into the ultimate nature of the mind and other phenomena. The Buddha likened shamatha to a great warrior who is needed to protect the wise minister of vipashyana.[109] After experimenting with various kinds of ascetic disciplines, this was a profound discovery made by the Buddha that swiftly led to his enlightenment. He later described this insight as follows:

> I thought of a time when my Sakyan father was working and I was sitting in the cool shade of a rose-apple tree: quite secluded from sensual desires disengaged from unwholesome things I had entered upon and abode in the first meditative stabilization, which is accompanied by coarse and precise investigation, with well-being and bliss born of seclusion. I thought: "Might that be

the way to enlightenment?" Then, following that memory, there came the recognition that this was the way to enlightenment.[110]

The distinction between access and the actual states of meditative stabilization is not made in the discourses of the Buddha as recorded in the Pali language, but first appears in the commentaries. Some Theravada Buddhists have claimed that *momentary* concentration *(khanika samadhi)* provides a sufficient basis in concentration for the perfection of vipashyana.[111] In the 1960s, a series of debates was held among Theravada Buddhist scholars, with one side arguing that the achievement of the first meditative stabilization is required to achieve liberation, and the other side arguing that momentary concentration is sufficient for vipashyana practice to fully liberate the mind.[112]

The contemporary Burmese meditation master Pa-Auk Tawya Sayadaw has concluded with considerable authority that access to the first meditative stabilization is a necessary and sufficient basis in samadhi for the perfect cultivation of contemplative insight. And he adds that the achievement of even the first meditative stabilization is very, very rare in today's world.[113] This assertion reflects the mainstream view of the Indian Mahayana tradition as well, namely that access concentration to the first meditative stabilization is the minimal degree of samadhi needed for vipashyana to be fully effective. This view is widely held among Tibetan Buddhists to this day.

The question of what degree of concentration is needed to liberate the mind irreversibly from its afflictive tendencies is best approached experientially, perhaps even scientifically. Both the Theravada and Mahayana traditions declare that the mind is irreversibly freed from mental afflictions only through the union of shamatha and vipashyana. Cognitive scientists may now be able to investigate these claims empirically, identifying the practices that result in such radical purification. Such an approach truly accords with the spirit of empiricism and pragmatism that has inspired the Buddhist tradition from its beginning.

CONCLUSION: A LOOK AHEAD ● ● ●

MODERN SCIENCE AND THE POTENTIAL OF SHAMATHA

The Buddhist "tree of knowledge" is grounded in the fertile soil of ethics, its root system is the mental balance achieved through the cultivation of focused attention, and its trunk is the wisdom achieved through the cultivation of contemplative insight. This is a radically different approach from modern science, which is considered to be value-free and driven by empirical data gathered with technological instruments and analyzed by mathematical reasoning. Physical science (including physics, chemistry, and biology) has provided us with knowledge about the external world, benefiting humanity with increased physical health and pleasures, while technologically tapping into the enormous potentials of matter and energy. Buddhist contemplative science, on the other hand, yields deep insights into the nature of consciousness, benefiting those who practice it with enhanced mental health and genuine happiness, while opening up the creative potentials of consciousness.

Each approach has its own strengths and weaknesses, and together they may be seen as complementary, rather than incompatible. In particular, while great advances have been made in the cognitive sciences in terms of the precise, third-person observation of the behavioral and neural correlates of mental states and activities, Buddhist contemplative science excels in the first-person, direct observation of mental phenomena. With its threefold method of ethics, shamatha, and vipashyana, the Buddhist approach provides

rigorous means to investigate the origins, nature, and potentials of consciousness, which have for the most part eluded scientific inquiry.

With the refined attention shamatha helps to cultivate, one may attain
various kinds of extrasensory perception and other paranormal abilities.
While Buddhist masters caution that seeking paranormal abilities can easily sidetrack one from the central endeavor of purifying the mind, these
abilities also can be put to good service for the benefit of others if they are
used with wisdom and altruism. Atisha comments in this regard:

> Just as a bird with undeveloped wings
> Cannot fly in the sky,
> Those without the power of extrasensory perception,
> Cannot work for the good of living beings.
>
> The merit gained in a single day
> By someone with extrasensory perception
> Cannot be gained even in a hundred lifetimes
> By one without extrasensory perception....
>
> Without the achievement of shamatha
> Extrasensory perception will not arise.
> Therefore make repeated effort
> To accomplish shamatha.[114]

The First Panchen Lama described the significance of shamatha for the
achievement of such abilities:

> Due to such practice, the nature of meditative equipoise is limpid
> and very clear, unobscured by anything. Since it is not estab-
> lished as any entity having form, it is vacuous like space, as it
> were. Moreover, whatever good and bad objects of the five senses
> arise, it clearly, luminously takes on any appearance, like the
> reflections in a limpid mirror. You have the sense that it cannot
> be recognized as being this and not being that. However stable

such samadhi may be, if it is not imbued with the joy of physical and mental pliancy, it is single-pointed attention of the desire realm, whereas samadhi that is so imbued is said to be shamatha; and that is the source of many qualities, such as extrasensory perception and paranormal abilities.[115]

Buddhist sources commonly list five mundane kinds of extrasensory perception:

1. Remote viewing, or clairvoyance
2. Clairaudience
3. Knowledge of others' minds
4. Paranormal abilities, such as the ability to mentally control the four elements of earth, water, fire, and air. Examples include moving through solid objects, walking on water, mental control of fire, flying, and mentally multiplying and transforming physical objects at will.
5. Recollection of past lives

Buddhist assertions regarding the possibilities of achieving extraordinary levels of sustained voluntary attention challenge the limits of current scientific understanding of the mind. If the paranormal abilities listed above look like sheer magic to us, who have grown accustomed to the materialistic biases of modern science, it is good to remember that the products of modern technology look just as much like magic to people from traditional societies where science has not been taught. No reasonable Buddhist would ask scientists to accept any of their claims merely on faith—the Buddha himself discouraged his followers from accepting his words simply on the basis of his authority—but it is equally dogmatic to dismiss them simply because they violate one's faith in scientific materialism.

The Dalai Lama comments in this regard, "A general basic stance of Buddhism is that it is inappropriate to hold a view that is logically inconsistent. This is taboo. But even more taboo than holding a view that is logically inconsistent is holding a view that goes against direct experience."[116]

It is equally illegitimate to reject out of hand something simply because one has not yet found compelling empirical evidence for it. Such evidence may be temporarily inaccessible only because the appropriate instrument for detecting it has not yet been developed. An open mind is crucial to both Buddhist and scientific inquiry, and more than that, it is vital to examine carefully issues that deeply challenge our most deep-rooted assumptions. Physicist Richard Feynman comments on this point:

> One of the ways of stopping science would be only to do experiments in the region where you know the law. But experimenters search most diligently, and with the greatest effort, in exactly those places where it seems most likely that we can prove our theories wrong. In other words, we are trying to prove ourselves wrong as quickly as possible, because only in that way can we find progress.[117]

A MEANINGFUL LIFE

The development of exceptional mental health and balance, free of all hindrances, is central to leading a meaningful life, which is far more significant than achieving paranormal abilities. Three elements appear to be crucial for the realization of a meaningful life: the pursuit of genuine happiness, truth, and virtue.

The Pursuit of Genuine Happiness

When thinkers like Saint Augustine, William James, or the Dalai Lama comment that the pursuit of genuine happiness is the meaning of life, they are obviously referring to something more than the pursuit of mere pleasure. They have in mind something deeper, a type of mental balance and equilibrium that carries us through the vicissitudes of life. Genuine happiness, which is a characteristic of human flourishing, is a symptom of a balanced, healthy mind, just as a sense of physical well-being is a sign of a healthy body. We have grown all too accustomed to the notion that suffering is inherent in life, that it is simply human nature for us to experience frustration, depression, anxiety, and misery. It is meaningful at times to experience sadness, for example, in response to the loss of a loved one or to human suffering as a result of a natural catastrophe. And we have evolved in such a way that fear can serve a useful function in helping us respond to danger. But on many occasions we experience a surplus of mental suffering that serves no good purpose at all. It is just a symptom of an unbalanced mind.

We may suffer due to following after desires that are detrimental to our own and others' well-being, as in the case of addiction. And it is debilitating to be unable to focus our attention at will, when the mind compulsively falls into one distraction after another, or simply fades into dullness. Difficulties of all kinds are bound to arise when we err in our perception of reality, either by failing to perceive things that clearly present themselves to us, or by confusing reality with our own projections and fantasies. And we may experience unnecessary turmoil by becoming overwhelmed with emotional imbalances, gyrating from excessive hope to fear, from elation to depression. The common symptom of all such mental imbalances is suffering. Just as we feel pain in the body when it is injured or ill, so do we experience mental distress when our minds are afflicted or unbalanced.

A meaningful life is oriented around the pursuit of genuine happiness that results from balancing the mind. The healthier the mind, the greater the sense of inner well-being. And a key to achieving exceptional states of mental health is the development of focused attention. Shantideva emphasized the importance of developing shamatha, cautioning that "a person whose mind is distracted lives between the fangs of mental afflictions."[118] When the mind is subject to attentional imbalances, it is as if one's psychological immune system is impaired, and so it can easily be overwhelmed by all kinds of mental afflictions.

The Pursuit of Truth

Though there are many kinds of knowledge, the most central to a meaningful life is knowledge and understanding that yield genuine happiness. According to Saint Augustine, the only thing we need to know is the answer to the question, "How can man be happy?"[119] This happiness he called "a truth-given joy," and for him, the only truth that can provide such happiness is divine. In Augustine's prayer, "May I know myself that I may know Thee," we hear an echo of Socrates' lament, "I am still unable, as the Delphic inscription orders, to know myself; and it really seems to me ridiculous to look into other things before I have understood that."[120]

There are many truths awaiting our discovery, much knowledge to be acquired, but what can be more important and more relevant to the pursuit of genuine happiness than insight into our own nature and our relation to the world around us? Central to this pursuit is the exploration of our own minds. While behavioral and neuroscientific research can indirectly tell us much about specific mental processes, for the study of the mind, William James declared that introspection is what we have to rely on first, foremost, and always.[121] This view has been expressed by contemplatives throughout the world, and for the introspective exploration of the depths of the human mind, focused attention is indispensable.

The Pursuit of Virtue

Aristotle equated genuine happiness with the "human good," declaring that it "comes to be disclosed as a being-at-work of the soul in accordance with virtue, and if the virtues are more than one, in accordance with the best and most complete virtue."[122] It is up to each of us, with our own belief systems and values, to identify what we regard as human virtues, and which ones are the best and most complete. A meaningful life is one that is focused on the cultivation of those virtues that we value in human life. Such a life will naturally be dedicated to overcoming mental traits and behavioral tendencies that are antithetical to such virtue, and for cultivation of virtue and the elimination of vices, the ability to focus the mind is crucial.

For all three of these elements of a meaningful life—the pursuit of genuine happiness, truth, and virtue—mental balance is needed. As you proceed on the path of shamatha, applying highly focused attention to the nature of consciousness itself, you may discover how deeply interrelated each of these pursuits are. There are dimensions of genuine happiness that can be fathomed only by means of self-discovery, there are truths that can be known experientially only within the context of a virtuous life, and there are virtues that may arise only as a result of gaining direct insight into the nature of reality. In a world in which the pursuits of happiness, truth, and virtue often appear unrelated or even at odds with each other, this integrated path may help unite the ancient and modern wisdom heritages of the East and the West.

APPENDIX:
SYNOPSIS OF THE NINE STAGES ● ● ●

	Step	What is achieved	The power by which that is achieved	What problems persist
1	Directed Attention	One is able to direct the attention to the chosen object	Learning the instructions	There is no attentional continuity on the object
2	Continuous Attention	Attentional continuity on the chosen object up to a minute	Thinking about the practice	Most of the time the attention is not on the object
3	Resurgent Attention	Swift recovery of distracted attention; mostly on the object	Mindfulness	One still forgets the object entirely for brief periods.
4	Close Attention	One no longer completely forgets the chosen object	Mindfulness, which is now strong	Some degree of complacency concerning samadhi
5	Tamed Attention	One takes satisfaction in samadhi	Introspection	Some resistance to samadhi
6	Pacified Attention	No resistance to training the attention	Introspection	Desire, depression, lethargy, and drowsiness
7	Fully Pacified Attention	Pacification of attachment, melancholy, and lethargy	Enthusiasm	Subtle imbalances of the attention, swiftly rectified
8	Single-pointed Attention	Samadhi is long, sustained without any excitation or laxity	Enthusiasm	It still takes effort to ward off excitation and laxity
9	Attentional balance	Flawless samadhi is long, sustained effortlessly	Familiarity	Attentional Imbalances may recur in the future

Coarse excitation: The attention completely disengages from the meditative object.

Medium excitation: Involuntary thoughts occupy the center of attention, while the meditative object is displaced to the periphery.

Subtle excitation: The meditative object remains at the center of attention, but involuntary thoughts emerge at the periphery of attention.

Attentional imbalances	The type of mental engagement	The quality of the experience	Involuntary thoughts
Coarse excitation	Focused	Movement	The flow of involuntary thought is like a cascading waterfall.
Coarse excitation	Focused	Movement	The flow of involuntary thought is like a cascading waterfall.
Coarse excitation	Interrupted	Movement	The flow of involuntary thought is like a cascading waterfall.
Coarse laxity and medium excitation	Interrupted	Achievement	Involuntary thoughts are like a river quickly flowing through a gorge.
Medium laxity and medium excitation	Interrupted	Achievement	Involuntary thoughts are like a river quickly flowing through a gorge.
Medium laxity and subtle excitation	Interrupted	Achievement	Involuntary thoughts are like a river slowly flowing through a valley.
Subtle laxity and excitation	Interrupted	Familiarity	Involuntary thoughts are like a river slowly flowing through a valley.
Latent impulses for subtle excitation and laxity	Uninterrupted	Stillness	The conceptually discursive mind is calm like an ocean with no waves.
The causes of those imbalances are still latent	Effortless	Perfection	The conceptually discursive mind is still like Mount Meru, king of mountains.

Coarse laxity: The attention mostly disengages from the object due to insufficient vividness.

Medium laxity: The object appears, but not with much vividness.

Subtle laxity: The object appears vividly, but the attention is slightly slack.

NOTES ● ● ●

1   William James, *The Principles of Psychology* (New York: Dover Publications, 1890/1958), II: 322.

2   James, *Talks to Teachers: On Psychology, and to Students on Some of Life's Ideals.* (New York: W. W. Norton, 1899/1958), p. 84.

3   James, *The Principles of Psychology,* I: 424.

4   This rendering is my own. See also *Ānāpānasati Sutta* in *The Middle Length Discourses of the Buddha,* Bhikkhu Bodhi, trans. (Boston: Wisdom Publications, 1995), pp. 943–44.

5   As cited in Tsong-kha-pa, *The Great Treatise on the Stages of the Path to Enlightenment,* The Lamrim Chenmo Translation Committee, trans. (Ithaca, NY: Snow Lion Publications, 2002), vol. 3, pp. 39–40.

6   *Satipaṭṭhāna Sutta,* in *The Middle Length Discourses of the Buddha,* p. 146.

7   See B. Alan Wallace, *Genuine Happiness: Meditation as the Path to Fulfillment* (Hoboken, NJ: John Wiley & Sons, 2005), chap. 1.

8   *Udāna* 47.

9   Śāntideva, *A Guide to the Bodhisattva Way of Life,* B. Alan Wallace & Vesna A. Wallace, trans. (Ithaca, NY: Snow Lion Publications, 1997), I: 28.

10 Geshe Rabten, *The Mind and Its Functions,* Stephen Batchelor, trans. (Mont Pèlerin, Switzerland: Edition Rabten, 2nd edition, 1992), pp. 74–75.

11 Daniel Kahneman, Ed Diener, and Norbert Schwarz, eds. *Well-being: The Foundations of Hedonic Psychology* (New York: Russell Sage Foundation, 1999).

12 For a more detailed account of loving-kindness meditation, see Sharon Salzberg, *Lovingkindness: The Revolutionary Art of Happiness* (Boston:

Shambhala Publications, 2002); Stephen G. Post, *Unlimited Love: Altruism, Compassion, and Service* (Philadelphia: Templeton Foundation Press, 2003); and B. Alan Wallace, *Genuine Happiness*, chap. 8.

13 *Sutra of the Ten Wheels of Kshitigarbha*, in Karma Chagmé, *A Spacious Path to Freedom: Practical Instructions on the Union of Mahāmudrā and Atiyoga*, Gyatrul Rinpoche, comm., B. Alan Wallace, trans. (Ithaca, NY: Snow Lion Publications, 1998), p. 77.

14 Paravahera Vajirañāṇa, *Buddhist Meditation in Theory and Practice* (Kuala Lumpur, Malaysia: Buddhist Missionary Society, 1975), p. 245.

15 Excerpted from *The Stages of the Listeners (Śāvakabhūmi)*.

16 Buddhadāsa Bhikkhu. *Mindfulness with Breathing: A Manual for Serious Beginners*. Santikaro Bhikkhu, trans. (Boston: Wisdom Publications, 1996).

17 *Udāna* I, 10.

18 For further reading on compassion, see Richard J. Davidson and Anne Harrington, eds., *Visions of Compassion: Western Scientists and Tibetan Buddhists Examine Human Nature* (New York: Oxford University Press, 2002); Lorne Ladner, *The Lost Art of Compassion: Discovering the Practice of Happiness in the Meeting of Buddhism and Psychology* (San Francisco: Harper San Francisco, 2004); and B. Alan Wallace, *Genuine Happiness*, chap. 9.

19 *Samyutta Nikāya* V, 321–22. *The Connected Discourses of the Buddha*, vol. II, Bhikkhu Bodhi, trans. (Boston: Wisdom Publications, 2000), p. 1774. I have altered the translation slightly.

20 Paravahera Vajirañāṇa, *Buddhist Meditation in Theory and Practice*, pp. 245–56.

21 Buddhaghosa, *The Path of Purification*. Bhikkhu Ñāṇamoli, trans. (Kandy: Buddhist Publication Society, 1979), VIII, 155.

22 Henry David Thoreau, *Walden*, Introduction by Basil Wiley (New York: W. W. Norton, 1951), p. 105.

23 Tsong-kha-pa, *The Great Treatise on the Stages of the Path to Enlightenment*, vol. 1, pp. 28–30.

24 *Aṅguttara Nikāya* V, 201ff.

25 This theme is discussed at length in H. H. the Dalai Lama, *Ethics for the New Millennium* (New York: Riverhead Books, 1999).

26 Geshe Sonam Rinchen, *Atisha's Lamp for the Path to Enlightenment*, Ruth

Sonam, trans. and ed. (Ithaca, NY: Snow Lion Publications, 1997), v. 39, p. 93. The translation of this verse published here is my own, slightly different from that in the above text.

27   Tsong-kha-pa, *The Great Treatise on the Stages of the Path to Enlightenment*, vol. 3, p. 76; B. Alan Wallace, *Balancing the Mind: A Tibetan Approach to Refining Attention* (Ithaca, NY: Snow Lion Publications, 2005), p. 192.

28   Geshe Rabten, *The Mind and Its Functions*, p. 62.

29   B. Alan Wallace, *Balancing the Mind*, p. 157.

30   Vasubandhu, *Abhidharmkośa*, 34.

31   Scott R. Bishop et al., "Mindfulness: A Proposed Operational Definition," *Clinical Psychology: Science and Practice*, 11:3, Fall 2004, p. 232.

32   Collett Cox, "Mindfulness and Memory: The Scope of *Smṛti* from Early Buddhism to the Sarvāstivādin Abhidharma," in *In the Mirror of Memory: Reflections on Mindfulness and Remembrance in Indian and Tibetan Buddhism*, Janet Gyatso, ed. (Albany: State University of New York, 1992), pp. 67–107.

33   Henepola Gunaratana, *Mindfulness in Plain English* (Boston: Wisdom Publications, 1991), p. 152.

34   *Saṃyutta Nikāya* V, 197–98.

35   *Milindapañha* 37–38; cf. R. M. L. Gethin, *The Buddhist Path to Awakening* (Oxford: Oneworld Publications, 2001), pp. 36–44.

36   Buddhaghosa, *The Path of Purification*, XIV, 141.

37   *Satipaṭṭhāna Sutta*.

38   Soma Thera, *The Way of Mindfulness: The Satipaṭṭhāna Sutta and Commentary* (Kandy, Sri Lanka: Buddhist Publication Society, 1975).

39   Buddhaghosa, *The Path of Purification*, VIII, 145–246.

40   B. Alan Wallace, *Balancing the Mind*, p. 150.

41   Karma Chagmé, *A Spacious Path to Freedom*, p. 77.

42   Henepola Gunaratana, *Mindfulness in Plain English*, p. 166.

43   Geshe Rabten, *The Mind and Its Functions*, p. 13.

44   *Majjhima Nikāya* 122, 15.

45   Buddhaghosa, *The Path of Purification*, IV, 172.

46   Asaṅga, *Mahāyānasūtrālaṃkāra*, Lévi, ed. and trans. (Paris: Bibliothèque de l'École des Hautes Études, 1907), 159 and 190, XIV, 13c–d. Cited in B. Alan Wallace, *Balancing the Mind*, p. 189.

47   Śāntideva, *A Guide to the Bodhisattva Way of Life*, V: 108.

48 D. J. Hacker, "Definitions and Empirical Foundations," in D. J. Hacker, J. Dunlosky, and A. C. Graesser, eds., *Metacognition in Educational Theory and Practice* (Mahwah, NJ: Erlbaum, 1998), pp. 1–24.

49 Padmasambhava, *Natural Liberation: Padmasambhava's Teachings on the Six Bardos*, Gyatrul Rinpoche, comm., B. Alan Wallace, trans. & ed. (Boston: Wisdom Publications, 1998), p. 102.

50 Collett Cox, "Mindfulness and Memory: The Scope of *Smṛti* from Early Buddhism to the Sarvāstivādin Abhidharma," pp. 71–72.

51 Düdjom Lingpa, *The Vajra Essence: From the Matrix of Primordial Consciousness and Pure Appearances, a Tantra on the Self-Arisen Nature of Existence*, B. Alan Wallace, trans. (Ashland, OR: Mirror of Wisdom Publications, 2004), p. 19.

52 Panchen Lozang Chökyi Gyaltsen, *Phyag rgya chen po'i rtsa ba*.

53 These are excerpted from Lerab Lingpa's commentary on the Dzogchen teachings called *Heart Essence of Vimalamitra*. Vimalamitra was a contemporary of Padmasambhava who also took a seminal role in bringing Buddhism to Tibet. Lerab Lingpa initially gave these instructions to a group of his close disciples, one of whom later wrote them down.

54 Lerab Lingpa (Gter ston las rab gling pa), *Lce btsun chen po'i vā ma la'i zab tig gi bshad khrid chu 'babs su bkod pa snying po'i bcud dril ye shes thig le*, Ven. Taklung Tsetrul Pema Wangyal, ed. (no publ. date), pp. 638–40.

55 Karma Chagmé, *A Spacious Path to Freedom*, pp. 68–72.

56 Düdjom Lingpa, *The Vajra Essence*, p. 287.

57 Ibid., pp. 23–26.

58 Ibid., p. 25.

59 Tenzin Wangyal Rinpoche, *Healing with Form, Energy and Light: The Five Elements in Tibetan Shamanism, Tantra, and Dzogchen*, Mark Dahlby, ed. (Ithaca, NY: Snow Lion Publications, 2002), pp. 13–20.

60 Düdjom Lingpa, *The Vajra Essence*, pp. 25–26.

61 Stephen LaBerge and Howard Rheingold, *Exploring the World of Lucid Dreaming* (New York: Ballantine, 1990); Stephen LaBerge, "Lucid Dreaming and the Yoga of the Dream State: A Psychophysiological Perspective," in *Buddhism & Science: Breaking New Ground*, B. Alan Wallace, ed. (New York: Columbia University Press, 2003), pp. 233–58.

62 Antonio Damasio, *The Feeling of What Happens: Body and Emotion in the Making of Consciousness* (New York: Harcourt, 1999), p. 320.

63 Werner Heisenberg, *Physics and Philosophy: The Revolution in Modern Science* (New York: Harper and Row, 1962), p. 58.

64 Asaṅga, *Mahāyānasūtrālaṃkāra*, Lévi, ed. and trans. (Paris: Bibliothèque de l'École des Hautes Études, 1907), 159 and 190, XIV, 13c–d. Cited in B. Alan Wallace, *Balancing the Mind*, p. 189.

65 H. H. the Dalai Lama & Alex Berzin, *The Gelug/Kagyü Tradition of Mahamudra* (Ithaca, NY: Snow Lion Publications, 1997), chap. 4.

66 *The Vajra Essence*, p. 23.

67 This citation is from the "Sems gnas pa'i thabs" section of his *Dge ldan bka' brgyud rin po che'i bka' srol phyag rgya chen po'i rtsa ba rgyas par bshad pa yang gsal sgron me*. Cf. "Saraha's Treasury of Songs," *Buddhist Texts through the Ages*, D. L. Snellgrove, trans., E. Conze, ed. (Oxford: Cassirer, 1954), vs. 70, p. 233.

68 Scott R. Bishop et al., "Mindfulness: A Proposed Operational Definition," *Clinical Psychology: Science and Practice*, 11:3, Fall 2004, p. 232.

69 Gunaratana, *Mindfulness in Plain English*, pp. 161, 165–66.

70 *Aṅguttara Nikāya* A. I, 8–10.

71 Düdjom Lingpa, *The Vajra Essence*, p. 46.

72 Stephen LaBerge, *Lucid Dreaming: A Concise Guide to Awakening in Your Dreams and in Your Life* (Boulder, CO: Sounds True, 2004), p. 14.

73 Ibid., p. 19.

74 Ibid., pp. 31–32.

75 Padmasambhava, *Natural Liberation*, pp. 105–9.

76 B. Alan Wallace, *The Taboo of Subjectivity: Toward a New Science of Consciousness* (New York: Oxford University Press, 2000), p. 142.

77 Daniel M. Wegner, *The Illusion of Conscious Will* (Cambridge, MA: MIT Press, 2002), pp. 341–42.

78 *Ratnameghasūtra*, cited in Śāntideva's *Śikṣāsamuccaya*, P. D. Vaidya, ed. (Darbhanga: Mithila Institute, 1961), p. 68.

79 This system of Sautrāntika philosophy is well presented in Anne Carolyn Klein, trans., *Knowing, Naming and Negation* (Ithaca, NY: Snow Lion Publications, 1991).

80 David Loy, *Nonduality: A Study in Comparative Philosophy* (New Haven: Yale University Press, 1988).

81 Jay L. Garfield, trans., *The Fundamental Wisdom of the Middle Way: Nāgārjuna's Mūlamadhyamakakārikā* (New York: Oxford University Press, 1995); Gen Lamrimpa, *Realizing Emptiness: Madhyamaka Insight Meditation*, B. Alan Wallace, trans. (Ithaca, NY: Snow Lion Publications, 2002); Michel Bitbol, "A Cure for Metaphysical Illusions: Kant, Quantum Mechanics, and Madhyamaka," in *Buddhism & Science*, B. Alan Wallace, ed., pp. 325–58.

82 Padmasambhava, *Natural Liberation*, pp. 142–43.

83 Tsongkhapa, *Small Exposition of the Stages of the Path*.

84 This citation is from the "Sems gnas pa'i thabs" section of his *Dge ldan bka' brgyud rin po che'i bka' srol phyag rgya chen po'i rtsa ba rgyas par bshad pa yang gsal sgron me*. Cf. Geshe Rabten, *Echoes of Voidness*, Stephen Batchelor, trans. and ed. (London: Wisdom Publications, 1986), pp. 113–28.

85 Deshung Rinpoche, *The Three Levels of Spiritual Perception*, Jared Rhoton, trans. (Boston: Wisdom Publications, 2003), p. 427.

86 *Saṃyutta Nikāya* II, 30.

87 Kamalaśīla, *First Bhāvanākrama*, in *Minor Buddhist Texts, Part II*, G. Tucci, ed. (Rome, 1958), p. 205.

88 Śāntideva, *A Guide to the Bodhisattva Way of Life*, VIII: 4.

89 Lecture on Mahamudra at the San Francisco Zen Center, 1976.

90 B. Alan Wallace, *Balancing the Mind*, p. 218.

91 Düdjom Lingpa, *The Vajra Essence*, p. 20.

92 Padmasambhava, *Natural Liberation*, pp. 152–62.

93 Padmasambhava, *Natural Liberation*, pp.113–14.

94 Paravahera Vajirañāṇa, *Buddhist Meditation in Theory and Practice* (Kuala Lumpur, Malaysia: Buddhist Missionary Society, 1975), p. 145.

95 Buddhaghosa, *The Path of Purification*, IV, 31.

96 *Majjhima Nikāya* I, 294–95.

97 Buddhaghosa, *The Path of Purification*, IV, 31.

98 *Saṃyutta Nikāya* II, 30.

99 *Dīgha Nikāya* I, 73–74.

100 Buddhaghosa, *The Path of Purification*, 126.

101 *Majjhima Nikāya* I, 33.

102 Buddhaghosa, *The Path of Purification*, 126.

103 Düdjom Lingpa, *The Vajra Essence*, p. 20.

104 *Saṃyutta Nikāya* II, 30.

105 Śāntideva, *A Guide to the Bodhisattva Way of Life*, VIII: 4.

106 B. Alan Wallace, *Balancing the Mind*, p. 118.

107 *Dīgha Nikāya* I, 73.

108 *Aṅguttara Nikāya* III, 63–64.

109 *Saṃyutta Nikāya* IV, 194–95.

110 *Majjhima Nikāya* 36, 85, 100.

111 *Paramatthamañjūsā* 278.

112 This debate is recorded on the following website: http://www.mahasi.org.mm/discourse/E24/E24ch01.htm

113 Ven. Pa-Auk Tawya Sayadaw, *Knowing and Seeing* (Kuala Lumpur, Malaysia: WAVE Publications, 2003) pp. 142, 186–87, 209.

114 Atīśa (Dīpaṃkaraśrījñāna), *Bodhipathapradīpa*. Sarat Chandra Das, ed., "Bodhipathapradīpa" *Journal of the Buddhist Text Society of India*, vol. 1., 1983, vv. 35–37.

115 This passage is at the conclusion of the "Sems gnas pa'i thabs" section of the *Dge ldan bka' brgyud rin po che'i bka' srol phyag rgya chen po'i rtsa ba rgyas par bshad pa yang gsal sgron me.*

116 Jeremy W. Hayward & Francisco J. Varela, eds., *Gentle Bridges: Conversations with the Dalai Lama on the Sciences of Mind* (Boston: Shambhala Publications, 1992), p. 37.

117 Richard Feynman, *The Character of Physical Law* (Cambridge, MA: MIT Press, 1965), p. 158.

118 Śāntideva, *A Guide to the Bodhisattva Way of Life*, VIII: 1.

119 Augustine, *Letters 100–155 (Epistolae)*, Roland Teske, trans. (Hyde Park NY: New City Press, 2003), 118: 13.

120 Plato, *Phaedo*. Robin Waterfield, trans. (New York: Oxford University Press, 2002), 230A.

121 William James, *The Principles of Psychology*, I: 185.

122 Aristotle, *Nicomachean Ethics*, Terence Irwin, trans. (Indianapolis: Hackett, 1985), 1098a16.

BIBLIOGRAPHY ● ● ●

Aristotle. *Nicomachean Ethics*. Translated by Terence Irwin. Indianapolis: Hackett Publication, 1985.

Augustine. *Letters 100–155 (Epistolae)*. Translated by Roland Teske. Hyde Park NY: New City Press, 2003.

Bhikkhu Bodhi, trans. *The Middle Length Discourses of the Buddha*. Boston: Wisdom Publications, 1995.

———. *The Connected Discourses of the Buddha*. 2 vols. Boston: Wisdom Publications, 2000.

Bishop, Scott R., et al. "Mindfulness: A Proposed Operational Definition." *Clinical Psychology: Science and Practice*, Vol. 11, No. 3, Fall 2004, pp. 230–41.

Bitbol, Michel. "A Cure for Metaphysical Illusions: Kant, Quantum Mechanics, and Madhyamaka." In *Buddhism & Science*, edited by B. Alan Wallace, pp. 325–58. New York: Columbia University Press, 2003.

Buddhadāsa. *Mindfulness with Breathing: A Manual for Serious Beginners*. Translated by Santikaro Bhikkhu. Boston: Wisdom Publications, 1996.

Buddhaghosa. *The Path of Purification*. Translated by Bhikkhu Ñāṇamoli. Kandy: Buddhist Publication Society, 1979.

Cox, Collett. "Mindfulness and Memory: The Scope of *Smṛti* from Early Buddhism to the Sarvāstivādin Abhidharma." In *In the Mirror of Memory: Reflections on Mindfulness and Remembrance in Indian and Tibetan Buddhism*, edited by Janet Gyatso, pp. 67–107. Albany: State University of New York, 1992.

H. H. the Dalai Lama. *Ethics for the New Millennium*. New York: Riverhead Books, 1999.

―――. *Dzogchen: The Heart Essence of the Great Perfection*. Translated by Geshe Thupten Jinpa and Richard Barron. Ithaca, NY: Snow Lion Publications, 2000.

H. H. the Dalai Lama and Alex Berzin. *The Gelug/Kagyü Tradition of Mahamudra*. Ithaca, NY: Snow Lion Publications, 1997.

Damasio, Antonio. *The Feeling of What Happens: Body and Emotion in the Making of Consciousness*. New York: Harcourt, 1999.

Davidson, Richard J., and Anne Harrington, eds. *Visions of Compassion: Western Scientists and Tibetan Buddhists Examine Human Nature*. New York: Oxford University Press, 2002.

Deshung Rinpoche. *The Three Levels of Spiritual Perception*. Translated by Jared Rhoton. Boston: Wisdom Publications, 2003.

Düdjom Lingpa. *The Vajra Essence: From the Matrix of Primordial Consciousness and Pure Appearances, a Tantra on the Self-Arisen Nature of Existence*. Translated by B. Alan Wallace. Ashland, OR: Mirror of Wisdom Publications, 2004.

Feynman, Richard. *The Character of Physical Law*. Cambridge, MA: MIT Press, 1965.

Flavell, John H. "Metacognitive Aspects of Problem Solving." In *The Nature of Intelligence*, edited by L. B. Resnick, pp. 231–36. Hillsdale, NJ: Erlbaum, 1976.

Garfield, Jay L., trans. *The Fundamental Wisdom of the Middle Way: Nāgārjuna's Mūlamadhyamakakārikā*. New York: Oxford University Press, 1995.

Gethin, R. M. L. *The Buddhist Path to Awakening*. Oxford: Oneworld Publications, 2001.

Gunaratana, Henepola. *Mindfulness in Plain English*. Boston: Wisdom Publications, 1991.

Hacker, D. J. "Definitions and Empirical Foundations." In *Metacognition in Educational Theory and Practice*, edited by D. J. Hacker, J. Dunlosky and A. C. Graesser, pp. 1–24. Mahwah, NJ: Erlbaum, 1998.

Harvey, Peter. *The Selfless Mind: Personality, Consciousness and Nirvana in Early Buddhism*. Surrey: Curzon Press, 1995.

Hayward, Jeremy W., and Francisco J. Varela, eds. *Gentle Bridges: Conversations with the Dalai Lama on the Sciences of Mind*. Boston: Shambhala Publications, 1992.

Heisenberg, Werner. *Physics and Philosophy: The Revolution in Modern Science*. New York: Harper and Row, 1962.

————. *Physics and Beyond: Encounters and Conversations*. New York: Harper and Row, 1971.

James, William. *The Principles of Psychology*. New York: Dover Publications, 1890/1958.

————. *Talks to Teachers: On Psychology; and to Students on Some of Life's Ideals*. New York: W. W. Norton, 1899/1958.

Kahneman, Daniel, Ed Diener, and Norbert Schwarz, eds. *Well-being: The Foundations of Hedonic Psychology*. New York: Russell Sage Foundation, 1999.

Kamalaśīla. *First Bhāvanākrama* in *Minor Buddhist Texts, Part II*. Edited by G. Tucci. Rome, 1958.

Karma Chagmé. *A Spacious Path to Freedom: Practical Instructions on the Union of Mahāmudrā and Atiyoga*. Commentary by Gyatrul Rinpoche. Translated by B. Alan Wallace. Ithaca, NY: Snow Lion Publications, 1998.

Klein, Anne Carolyn, trans. *Knowing, Naming and Negation*. Ithaca, NY: Snow Lion Publications, 1991.

LaBerge, Stephen. "Lucid Dreaming and the Yoga of the Dream State: A Psychophysiological Perspective." In *Buddhism & Science*, edited by B. Alan Wallace, pp. 233–58. New York: Columbia University Press, 2003.

————. *Lucid Dreaming: A Concise Guide to Awakening in Your Dreams and in Your Life*. Boulder, CO: Sounds True, 2004.

LaBerge, Stephen, and Howard Rheingold. *Exploring the World of Lucid Dreaming*. New York: Ballantine, 1990.

Ladner, Lorne. *The Lost Art of Compassion: Discovering the Practice of Happiness in the Meeting of Buddhism and Psychology*. San Francisco: Harper San Francisco, 2004.

Lamrimpa, Gen. *Realizing Emptiness: Madhyamaka Insight Meditation*. Translated by B. Alan Wallace. Ithaca, NY: Snow Lion Publications, 2002.

Lati and Lochö Rinbochay, L. Zahler, and J. Hopkins. *Meditative States in Tibetan Buddhism: The Concentrations and Formless Absorptions*. London: Wisdom Publications, 1983.

Loy, David. *Nonduality: A Study in Comparative Philosophy*. New Haven: Yale University Press, 1988.

Nyanaponika Thera. *The Heart of Buddhist Meditation*. New York: Samuel Weiser, 1973.

Padmasambhava. *Natural Liberation: Padmasambhava's Teachings on the Six Bardos*. Commentary by Gyatrul Rinpoche. Translated and edited by B. Alan Wallace. Boston: Wisdom Publications, 1998.

Plato. *Phaedo*. Translated by Robin Waterfield. New York: Oxford University Press, 2002.

Posner, Michael I. *Foundations of Cognitive Science*. Cambridge, MA: MIT Press, 1989.

Post, Stephen G. *Unlimited Love: Altruism, Compassion, and Service*. Philadelphia: Templeton Foundation Press, 2003.

Rabten, Geshe. *Echoes of Voidness*. Translated and edited by Stephen Batchelor. London: Wisdom Publications, 1986.

———. *The Mind and Its Functions*. Translated by Stephen Batchelor, 2nd ed. Mont Pèlerin, Switzerland: Edition Rabten, 1992.

Salzberg, Sharon. *Lovingkindness: The Revolutionary Art of Happiness*. Boston: Shambhala Publications, 2002.

Śāntideva. *A Guide to the Bodhisattva Way of Life*. Translated by B. Alan Wallace & Vesna A. Wallace. Ithaca, NY: Snow Lion Publications, 1997.

Searle, John R. *Mind: A Brief Introduction*. New York: Oxford University Press, 2004.

Snellgrove, D. L., trans. "Saraha's Treasury of Songs." In *Buddhist Texts through the Ages*, edited by E. Conze. Oxford: Cassirer, 1954.

Sonam Rinchen, Geshe. *Atisha's Lamp for the Path to Enlightenment*. Translated and edited by Ruth Sonam. Ithaca: NY: Snow Lion Publications, 1997.

Tenzin Wangyal Rinpoche. *Healing with Form, Energy and Light: The Five Elements in Tibetan Shamanism, Tantra, and Dzogchen*. Edited by Mark Dahlby. Ithaca, NY: Snow Lion Publications, 2002.

Thoreau, Henry David. *Walden*. New York: W. W. Norton, 1951.

Tsong-kha-pa. *The Great Treatise on the Stages of the Path to Enlightenment*. Translated by The Lamrim Chenmo Translation Committee. Ithaca, NY: Snow Lion Publications, 2002.

Vajirañāṇa, Paravahera. *Buddhist Meditation in Theory and Practice*. Kuala Lumpur, Malaysia: Buddhist Missionary Society, 1975.

Wallace, B. Alan. *The Taboo of Subjectivity: Toward a New Science of Consciousness*. New York: Oxford University Press, 2000.

—————. ed. *Buddhism and Science: Breaking New Ground*. New York: Columbia University Press, 2003.

—————. *Balancing the Mind: A Tibetan Approach to Refining Attention*. Ithaca, NY: Snow Lion Publications, 2005.

—————. *Genuine Happiness: Meditation as the Path to Fulfillment*. Hoboken, NJ: John Wiley & Sons, 2005.

Wegner, Daniel M. *The Illusion of Conscious Will*. Cambridge, MA: MIT Press, 2002.

Wilson, E. O. *Consilience: The Unity of Knowledge*. New York: Alfred A. Knopf, 1998.

INDEX

ABOUT WISDOM PUBLICATIONS ● ● ●

Wisdom Publications, a nonprofit publisher, is dedicated to making available authentic Buddhist works for the benefit of all. We publish translations of the sutras and tantras, commentaries and teachings of past and contemporary Buddhist masters, and original works by the world's leading Buddhist scholars. We publish our titles with the appreciation of Buddhism as a living philosophy and with the special commitment to preserve and transmit important works from all the major Buddhist traditions.

If you would like more information or a copy of our mail order catalog, please write or call us at this address:

Wisdom Publications
199 Elm Street
Somerville, Massachusetts, 02144 USA
Tel: (617) 776-7416 • Fax: (617) 776-7841
www.wisdompubs.org • info@wisdompubs.org

Wisdom Publications is a nonprofit, charitable 501(c)(3) organization and a part of the Foundation for the Preservation of the Mahayana Tradition (FPMT).

In the Buddha's Words
An Anthology of Discourses
from the Pali Canon
Edited and introduced by Bhikkhu Bodhi
Foreword by the Dalai Lama
512 pages, ISBN 0-86171-491-1, $18.95

This is the definitive introduction to the Buddha's teachings—in his own words. The American scholar-monk Bhikkhu Bodhi, whose translations have won widespread acclaim, here presents selected discourses of the Buddha from the Pali Canon, the earliest record of what the Buddha taught. *In the Buddha's Words* reveals the full scope of the Buddha's discourses, from family life and marriage to renunciation and the path of insight. A concise introduction precedes each chapter, guiding the reader toward a deeper understanding of the texts that follow.

Taken as a whole, these texts bear eloquent testimony to the breadth and intelligence of the Buddha's teachings, and point the way to an ancient yet ever-vital path. Students and seekers alike will find this systematic presentation indispensable.

Sleeping, Dreaming, and Dying
An Exploration of Consciousness
His Holiness the Dalai Lama
254 pages, ISBN 0-86171-123-8, $16.95

"A most stimulating and informative work. By successfully balancing the specialized technical perspectives of science and philosophy (both Euro-American and Tibetan) with the more practical concerns of everyday life, and death, *Sleeping, Dreaming, and Dying* offers important insights for those genuinely interested in meaningful contacts between Buddhism, psychology, and neuroscience."—*Tibet Journal*

Tibetan Buddhism from the Ground Up
A Practical Approach for Modern Life
B. Alan Wallace
228 pages, ISBN 0-86171-075-4, $15.95

This highly readable book asks neither unquestioning faith nor blind obedience to abstract concepts or religious beliefs. Rather, it challenges us to investigate life's issues for ourselves in the light of an ancient and effective approach to the sufferings and joys of the human condition.

"One of the most readable, accessible, and comprehensive introductions to Tibetan Buddhism."—*Mandala*

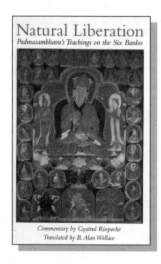

Natural Liberation
Padmasambhava's Teachings on the Six Bardos
Padmasambhava
Commentary by Gyatrul Rinoche
Translated by B. Alan Wallace
272 pages, ISBN 0-86171-131-9, $16.95

Padmasambhava, the great eighth-century Indian master who established Buddhism in Tibet, describes in detail six life-processes, or *bardos*, and how to transform them into vehicles for enlightenment. This most extraordinary teaching is here accompanied by meditation instructions and edifying anecdotes in a lucid commentary by Gyatrul Rinpoche, an esteemed teacher of the Nyingma tradition.

MindScience
An East-West Dialogue
His Holiness the Dalai Lama, Herbert Benson, Robert A.F. Thurman,
Howard E. Gardner, Daniel Goleman
152 pages, ISBN 0-86171-066-5, $14.95

"The Dalai Lama synthesizes scientific materialism and Western psychology with the ancient mind of the Buddha—without any apparent contradiction. Other notable scholars contribute to the discussion. *MindScience* captures the spirit of genuine inquiry and offers a glimpse of Buddhist psychology and its potential applications in the West today."—*Tricycle*

"A lively and interesting description of the dynamic interaction between Buddhism and mainstream science...full of pearls."—*Shambhala Sun*

Meditation & Relaxation in Plain English
Bob Sharples
208 pp, ISBN 0-86171-286-2, $14.95

Quite simply, *Meditation and Relaxation in Plain English* is the clearest, broadest, and most friendly book available for who would like to feel less stress—and more ease and joy—in life.

"I can recommend it without hesitation or qualification to all those who seek information about meditation but who are turned off by proselytizing! You can bet it will be on the recommended book list I offer my students."
—Frank Jude Boccio, author of *Mindfulness Yoga*